National Cooperative Organisations in India

National Cooperative Organisations in India

Dr. Lamaan Sami

AKANSHA PUBLISHING HOUSE
NEW DELHI • GUWAHATI • VISAKHAPATNAM

AKANSHA PUBLISHING HOUSE
4649-B/21, Ansari Road
Darya Ganj, New Delhi - 110 002
Ph.: 23263193 / 9811582579 / 09435116718
Fax: 011-23263193
Email: ektabooks@yahoo.com
www.akanshapublishinghouse.com

National Cooperative Organisations in India

First Published 2012
ISBN 978-81-8370-312-3

PRINTED IN INDIA

Published by Akansha Publishing House, New Delhi and Printed at Harmain Offset, Delhi.

Dedicated

to

Late Choudhary Brahm

Prakash ji
a Doyen of Indian

Cooperative Movement

Contents

Preface

Cooperatives came into existence to help the poor rural masses as well as to serve the purpose of British Government. The ideal situation for its development as a democratic movement could not be established as it was nourished under the guidance of Britain Born Registrar who worked as monarch of cooperative system.

After Independence cooperation was visualized as an essential instrument for achieving people aspiration in order to establish socio-economic equality. The Planning Commission started formulating Five-year Plans of National Development and Cooperation was given a vital role to secure peoples participation in the formulation and implementation of plans for their own development.

The father of nation Mahatma Gandhi saw a great virtue in cooperation as an instrument of rural development. He assigned specific roles to cooperatives in the field of agriculture, recommending the promotion of cooperative farming and thereby preventing further fragmentation of landholdings. He also advocated the establishment of other types of non-credit cooperatives such as weavers' and spinners' cooperatives and dairy cooperatives etc. Jawaharlal Nehru the first Prime Minister of India, also had a strong faith in the cooperatives. He wanted India to be 'convulsed with the cooperative movement'. He considered cooperatives as a pillar of economic democracy imbued with the basic values of voluntaries, autonomy, social cohesion and flexibility. World has seen two economic systems in operation i.e, capitalism and socialism. The world, however wants the best of the Cooperation; being a way of life it can do a lot of good to human beings.

Thus during planning period much emphasis was laid on the expansion and diversification of the cooperative movement. In order to solve the problem of rural poverty and backwardness almost all types of cooperative societies were organized and developed during Nehruvian period. In order to establish the cooperatives in all walks of life it was necessary to develop their organizational structure. According to sixth principle of cooperative as laid down by ICA Cooperatives serve their members most effectively and strength the cooperative movement by working together through local, national, regional and international structures. Thus, Federation existence is necessary to strengthen primaries and district as well as state and national level organization (bottom up approach). In India a beginning in this direction was made with the establishment of NAFED the First National Level Cooperative Federation followed by others. Today 17 National Level Cooperative Organizations exist and work for the welfare of the society. The primary aim of all Federations is alleviation of poverty, inclusive growth and financial inclusion with emphasis an empowerment of women.

As a whole the cooperative movement has served/serving the nation and upheld the values of financial inclusiveness and sustainable progress. A sad commentary is that the Five-year Plan document now does not give same place to cooperatives as it had given during Nehruvian period although they are playing more important role in all segments of society particularly empowerment of women and alleviation of poverty from rural India. The government should consider it seriously, and invite a debate on this issue before launching

12th Five-year Plan. Also the government should look into the problems of cooperatives and provide logistic support for their good health.

I have drawn heavily upon various standard publications, including research papers and reports of Seminars, Conferences, Congresses as well as reports of committees and commissions appointed by the government. I am greatful to all learned authors namely; Messrs J.B. Bhanot, T.T. Adkhari, K.K. Ravindra, M.L. Khurana, S.J. Sequeri, Vinay Kumar, B. Subrahmanryam, B. Krishnia, R. N. Pandey, P.K. Shrawat, K. V. Thomas, M. M. Tewary, Mr. R. N. Pandey, and Dr. U.S. Awasthi, Dr. Ravi Shankar, Dr. R. N. Ghotak, and Dr. Dewedi whose works have been quoted.

I am grateful to my teachers viz., Prof. S. U. Farooqui, Dean, Faculty of Commerce, Prof. Z. U. Khairoowala, Chairman, Department of Commerce, Prof. Badar Alam Iqbal, Prof. Javed Alam Khan, Prof. Mahfoozur Rehman, Dr. Sheeba Hamid and other colleagues who have provided help to me.

I feel proud of my father Prof. Samiuddin, a visionary cooperator who has inspired me to work on this project and provided necessary guidance in completing it.

I also place on record the good wishes and necessary help provided by Mr. Mohan Misra, Editor (Cooperator), Mrs. Anita Manchanda, Chief Executive of NCUI, Mr. B. D. Sharma ICA, Ms. Sabitha Venkatesam, Librarian NCUI, Dr. V. K. Dubey and Mrs. Sonika Nayyer.

Last but not the least, I offer my thanks to those who remained unmentioned but their writings and good wishes have contributed a lot towards the completion of this work.

I would feel amply rewarded if this work stimulates further thinking, discussion and research in this field.

Dr. Lamaan Sami

1

National Cooperative Union of India (NCUI)

The cooperative movement was introduced in India in 1904 and the National Cooperative Union of India, an apex body of cooperatives took birth after 25 years. Being the apex organization of the Indian Cooperative Movement it will be interesting for researchers to know the origin of National Cooperative Union of India (NCUI) which goes back to the year 1929 when All India Provincial Cooperative Institutes Association came into being with Shri Lallubhao Samldas as its President.

In the early years the primary societies were established in large numbers and soon the need was felt for federal organizations at the district and the state level to serve them. By the end of 1920, most of provinces in British India had a Provincial Cooperative Bank in accordance with the recommendation of Maclagen Committee. The cooperatives also established provincial cooperative Institutes in different provinces which were holding respective provincial level conferences to discuss their issues and evolve a common consensus. The principal functions of the provincial institutes were imparting cooperative education, building the image of cooperatives and serving as a liason body between the cooperative department and honorary workers upon whose ability the success of cooperation depended. These provincial level conference felt the need to forge an All India Cooperative Organization. Crystallization of this idea occurred at the first meeting of the Apex Cooperative Banks which was convened at the instance of Bihar and Orissa Provincial Cooperative Bank and the Bombay Provincial Cooperative Bank. At this conference a decision was taken to establish an Association of the Indian Provincial Cooperative Banks with a Standing Committee composed of the representatives of each of the member bank. This led to the formation of Indian Provincial Cooperative Banks Association, with Sir Lallubhai Samaldas as President and Shri V. C. Rangaswamy as Secretary.[1]

The scope of the Indian Provincial Cooperative Banks' Association was circumscribed to protection, furtherance and representation of common interests in finance, legislations, administration, development of the member banks, and convening of periodal conferences. Still all the problems of the movement were not discussed and the need for an All India Cooperative Organization continued to be felt. In March, 1928, Shri V. Ramadas Pantuly, President of the Madras Provincial Cooperative Union harped on the need to provide a suitable leadership for the movement by communicating with all the provincial cooperative institutes in the country in this direction. A suggestion was mooted that in course of time the standing committee of this conference could form the nucleus of an all Indian cooperative organization. The proposal was welcomed by the provincial institutes resulting in the convening of First All India Cooperative Institutes Conference at Simla in September 1928 under the presidentship of Shri Lallubhai Samaldas, along with the second Indian Provincial Cooperative Banks' Conference presided over by Shri V. Ramadas Pantulu. The conference considered the question of establishing an All

India Provincial Cooperative Institute Association but felt it desirable to consult all the institutes before finally deciding on the aims, objects and constitution of the association. A Standing Committee with Shri V. Ramadas Pantulu as Chairman and Shri V. L. Mehta, Shri S. K. Lanin, Rai bahadur N. K. Kelkar and Khan Mohammad Basher Khan was appointed to draft a scheme for constitution of the Association. The conference was adjourned and met later in September, 1929 when it adopted the Constitution of the Association. Shri Lallubhai have suggested a single All India Cooperative Conference to which the provincial and princely state governments were to be invited to depute their Registrars of Cooperative Societies.[2]

The first joint conference was held at Amravati in June 1934 under the Presidentship of Sir Lallubhai Samaldas. It was at this conference that Shri V. Ramadas Pantulu, who as already elected President of Indian Provincial Cooperative Banks' Association was elected President of Institute's Association. This development on the leadership firstly in the hands of Shri Pantulu and later in Prof. H. L. Kaji facilitated in strengthening both the organizations. It led to their coordinate working. In order to give a cohesive and organized orientation to the working process, the President. All India Cooperative Union, Prof. H. L. Kaji in his Presidential address to the 6th All India Conference held at Lucknow in 1946 expressed the view that two conferences – one of the cooperators with a few cooperative Registrars and the other of cooperative officials with a few cooperators-to some extent, duplicate each other. He felt that the better step would be to have an All India Cooperative Congress meeting once in a year where Registrars of provinces and states and representatives of provincial cooperative organizations attend as members. The conference resolved that there should be one conference instead of two-one of officials and the other of non-officials. Another notable event of this conference was that Khan Mohammad Bashir Ahmad Khan who was the secretary of the All India Cooperative Institutes' Association only till then was elected Secretary of both the association. In this manner link was forged towards the path of centralization. The cooperative opinion was veering around the ideal of evolving a national cooperative authority in a slow manner.[3]

The resolution of the Congress was not considered by the Government in a favourable manner and a Registrar's conference was convened to be held at Madras in May, 1947 to consider the recommendations of the cooperative Planning Committee. The All India Cooperative Conference was also convened to be held at Madras a few days before the date of the Registrars' Conference to consider the report of the Planning Committee. In his presidential address to this conference Prof. H. L. Kaji made a vigorous plea for the amalgamation of these two conferences. He was of the view that it was waste of time, money and effort to have two conferences where more or less the same set of people meet together to consider the problems and policies of the same movement. The appeal of the President had its immediate effect as the conference passed a resolution requesting the office bearers of the two All India Association to prepare a scheme for evolving an All India Cooperative Association. The office-bearers proceeded to implement this decision and prepared a constitution for new All India Organization that would result from the amalgamation of both the associations.[4]

The Registrar's conference which was held a few days later considered the proposal of amalgamation of the two conferences and recommended to the Government to appoint a committee to find a workable solution suggest ways and means for implementing this recommendation. The government of India then appointed a special sub-committee on cooperation under the Chairmanship of Shri R. G. Saraiya which recommended to the Government for the amalgamation of the two conference. The committee favoured the idea of a single cooperative body at the national level representing the entire cooperative movement and recommended that this Association should be given liberal grant by the Central Government. [5]

Meanwhile, the two association had decided to have a single cooperative association and the office-bearers had prepared a constitution for this in accordance with the resolution of the All India Cooperative Conference held at Madras in May, 1947. In this scenario the 8th All India Cooperative Conference held at Bangalore in May, 1949 under the Presidentship of Prof. H. L. Kaji adopted the constitution of the Indian Cooperative Union. *The Indian Cooperative Union came into being on 15th May, 1949.* Prof. H. L. Kaji was elected as its President and Shri B. J. Patel as its Hon. General Secretary. It was later renamed as the *All India Cooperative Union in 1954.* Again in **1961** the name was changed and now it is known as *National Cooperative Union of India* with its office at 3, Institutional Area, August Keranti Marg, New Delhi.[6]

In short the NCUI has travelled a long way since then to emerge as the sole representative of the cooperative movement in the country. Being the apex organization of the Indian cooperative movement in the country, the NCUI is committed to lend dynamism and vibrancy to the cooperative sector in the twenty first century. At present it has 202 members consisting of 17 National level Federations, 147 State level agencies and 38 Multi-State cooperatives. The membership of NCUI comprises of cooperative institutions of national level, state level and multi-state cooperative societies. These institutions represent different sectors of the Indian Cooperative Movement. There are 204 Cooperative Institutions as members of NCUI. Category-wise break up of the Member Institutions of NCUI, is as follows:

1.	National Level Cooperative Federations	17
2.	State Cooperative Unions	27
3.	Cooperative Unions of Union Territories	04
4.	State Cooperative Marketing Federations	16
5.	State Cooperative Banks	18
6.	State Cooperative Agricultural and Rural Development Banks	14
7.	State Cooperative Consumer's Federations	08
8.	State Coop. House Building/Housing Finance Societies	10
9.	State Federation of Urban Cooperative Banks and Credit Societies	10
10.	Other State Cooperative Federations	
	* Dairy/Milk Marketing Federations	08
	* Handloom/Industrial	05
	* Sugar/Cane Federations	05
	* Spinning Mills Federations	03
	* State Cooperative Banks Associations	02
	* Miscellaneous	17
11.	State Tribal Cooperative Development Corporation/ Federation	02
12.	Multi-State Cooperative Societies	38[7]

The main objectives of these organizations are to popularize the cooperative principles, cooperative ideology and cooperative values, to organize cooperative education and training programmes, convene Indian Cooperative Congress, Seminars, Meetings, Workshops, Conferences and Exhibitions; select delegates on behalf of the Union to participate in International, National and State Conference, lobbying with Government of India and State Government, Image building through publicity and public relations, to conduct IT training programmes and to bring out publications.

An important activity of the NCUI is Human resource development through cooperative education and training. The National Council for training looks up the training programme. Moreover, five regional institutes of corporative management, 14 Institutes of cooperative management and 109 cooperative training centres of state cooperative union are engaged in doing this work.

To strengthen the cooperative movement NCUI takes necessary reports namely:

1. Democratisation and Professionalisation of Cooperative Movement
2. Lobbying with State Governments and Government of India
   a. to ensure timely elections in Cooperatives;
   b. to Amend Cooperative Laws to provide Greater Autonomy to Coops and ensure their functioning in accordance of cooperative principles;
3. Influencing the Cooperative Organizations to have well defined Manpower Development and Professional policies;
4. Tailoring the cooperative education and training programme based on requirements of cooperative organization.

It supporting State Cooperative Unions:

1. Monitoring and Guidance of Member Education Programmes;
2. Supply of Education Materials;
3. Refresher Courses for Instructors;

4. JTC Faculty Development Programmes;
5. Financial Assistance for Seminars, conferences, Study Visit and JTC Development.

At present the Union is looking into the necessary law reforms for a healthy future of cooperative in a new free environment. Some structural and institutional reforms are also under consideration. To make cooperatives independent and free from Government interference is necessary for which they should be made self sufficient.

Imparting cooperative education to office bearers, members and employees of various cooperative societies is one of the major activities of NCUI. These activities are carried out through the following:

1. National Centre for Cooperative Education (NCCE), New Delhi
2. NCUI Cooperative Education Field Projects;
3. NCUI Cooperative Educational Field Projects exclusive for Women;
4. NCUI Cooperative Education Field Projects in North Eastern States;
5. Monitoring and Guidance to Cooperative Education Activities being carried out by State Cooperative Unions.[8]

Main Functions

National Cooperative Union of India

- Promotion and Strengthening of Cooperative Sector;
- Strengthening of Human Resource Development in Cooperatives (HRD) through (i) Cooperative Education and (ii) Cooperative Training
- Network Development of Cooperative Information System and Extending Services;

Summary of Organisational Stucture, Functions and Progress*

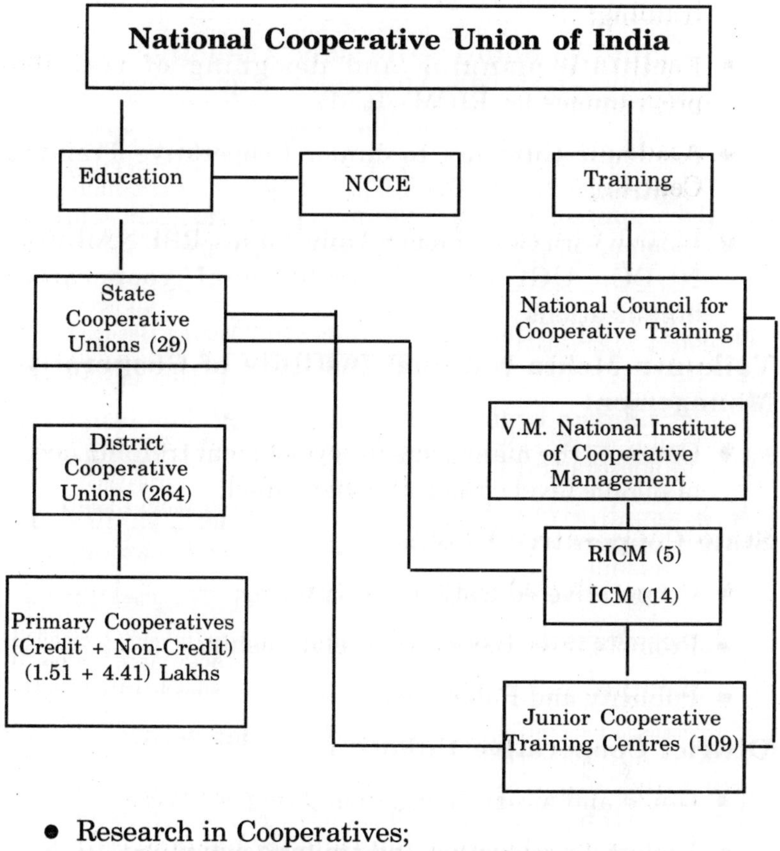

- Research in Cooperatives;
- Propagation of Cooperative Ideology;
- Lobbying and Image Building Through; (i) Cooperative Parliamentarians' Forum (ii) Publication and Publicity
- International Cooperative Relations;
- Cooperative Planning;

*Indian Cooperative Movement—A Statistical Profile-2009, pp. 84-85

National Council for Cooperative Training

- Research in cooperation;
- Formulate policies and plans relating to cooperative training;
- Facilitate planning and designing of training programmes for RICM's/ICM's.
- Academic Guidance to Junior Cooperative Training Centres;
- Liasion with Government, Universities, RBI, NABARD, NCDC, UGC and Inter-national cooperative organizations;

Vaikunth Mehta National Institute of Cooperative Management

- Caters to the management/development training needs of middle level cooperative personnel;

State Cooperative Unions

- Cooperative education and training;
- Promote inter-cooperative relationship;
- Publicity and Publications;

District Cooperative Unions

- Guide and assist in organizing cooperatives;
- Undertake education and training activities;

Junior Training Centres

- Arrange training of Junior level cooperative personnel

Approach

With a view to ensure appropriate positioning of cooperatives in the emerging liberalized competitive economy, the following strategy has been formulated and is currently under implementation. It is as follows:

- Implementation of National Cooperative Policy;
- Promotion of Cooperation among cooperatives and to develop coordination between cooperatives;
- Strengthening base level cooperative Institutions by promoting the use of ICT application
- Enhancing Involvement of rural poor in the cooperative movement by organizing them into Self-help Groups and activising membership of cooperatives;
- Networking of Cooperative Information System;
- To achieve self-sufficiency by strengthening the resources;

New Areas

- To establish Jawahar Lal Nehru International Cooperative University;
- Set-up COOP CONNECT Forum to popularize cooperative model of development;
- Human Resource Development [9]

NOTES

1. Quoted from NCUI, *Cooperator Vol. XXXVI,* No. 10, April, 1999, pp. 382-385.
2. *Ibid.*
3. *Ibid.*
4. *Ibid.*
5. *Ibid.*
6. *Ibid.*
7. NCUI, *Annual Report 2009-2010,* "Management and Administration of NCUI", NCUI, New Delhi, 110 016, p. 1.

8. NCUI, *Annual Report 2009-2010,* Cooperative Education, NCUI, New Delhi, 110 016, p. 3.
9. *Indian Cooperative Movement—A Statistical Profile-2009,* pp. 84-85.

2

National Agricultural Cooperative Marketing Federation of India Ltd. (NAFED)

India has gone through a green revolution, white revolution and now passing through yellow revolution. The Government of India seeks to promote agriculture development and research programme to meet the challenges in India agriculture and to arrest decelerating trends in capital formation in agriculture and step up public investment to accelerate development of supportive infrastructure for agriculture and rural development. With these objectives in view, the National Agricultural Policy was formulated to actualize the vast untapped growth potential of Indian agriculture, strengthen rural infrastructure to support faster agriculture development, promote value addition, accelerate the growth of agro business, create employment in rural areas, secure a fair standard of living for the farmers so as to face the challenges arising out of economic liberalization and globalization.[1]

Cooperative marketing societies came into existence after 1912 Act, but a real progress was made during the plan period. These societies under take the functions of supply of agricultural produce, inputs, commercial articles and storage facilities.

The cooperative structure in India is of three tiers with NAFED as national organization and 27 State level cooperative marketing federations, 3216 General purpose primary marketing societies and 5585 special commodities societies.

NAFED was established by Government of India on October 2nd, 1958 as an Apex Institution for Marketing Cooperatives in the country with the prime objective to provide regular market support to farmers by ensuring reasonable price for their produce. For over five decades, NAFED has been rendering varied and valuable services to the farmers by performing activities in the following areas:

- Providing market support to farmers through its commercial purchases.
- Acting as the Central Nodal Agency of the Government of India for undertaking purchases of oilseeds and pulses under Price Support Scheme.
- Acting as the agency of the Government of India for making purchases under Market Intervention Scheme.
- Acting as the canalizing agency of the Government of India for select commodities.
- Assisting farmers to source various agriculture inputs.[2]

NAFED undertakes purchase of various agricultural commodities directly from the farmers and through the involvement of State Cooperative Marketing Federations at state level and primary Cooperative Marketing Societies at village level. No middlemen is involved by NAFED while making the purchases.

The business turnover of NAFED during the last 5 years can be read from the following figure 2.1.

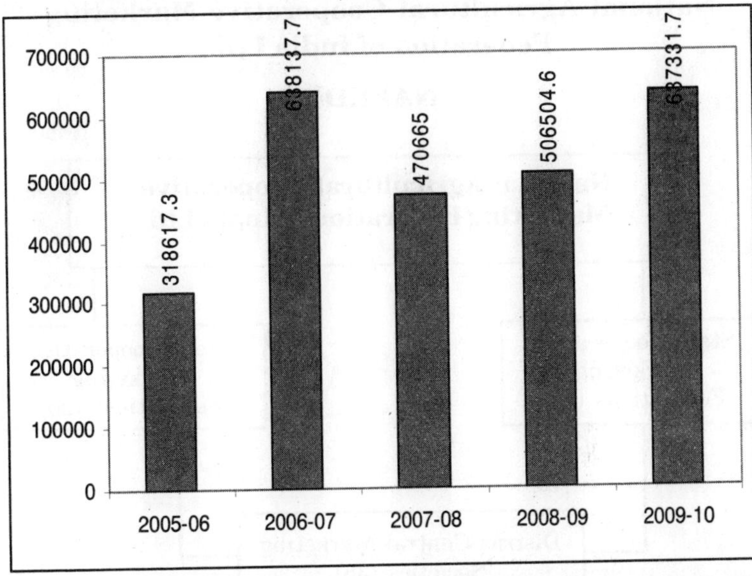

Figure 2.1: The Business Turnover of NAFED (2005-06 to 2009-10)

NAFED achieved turnover of Rs. 5735.33 crores during 2009-10 in outright account, in addition, a turnover of Rs. 6.89 crores was achieved agency/consignment business and Rs. 631.10 crores was achieved through export of onion by associate shippers. Against this, the turnover during the last year was Rs. 5065.05 crores.

There was a record Gross Profit of Rs. 83.91 crores, almost similar to last year's but due to huge interest liability on account of outstanding loans in Tie-Up business, there was a net loss of Rs. 50.06 crores.[3]

Main Functions

National Agricultural Cooperative Marketing Federation

- Marketing of agricultural produce in the country;

Summary of Organisational Structure, Functions and Progress*

National Agricultural Cooperative Marketing Federation of India Ltd.

NAFED

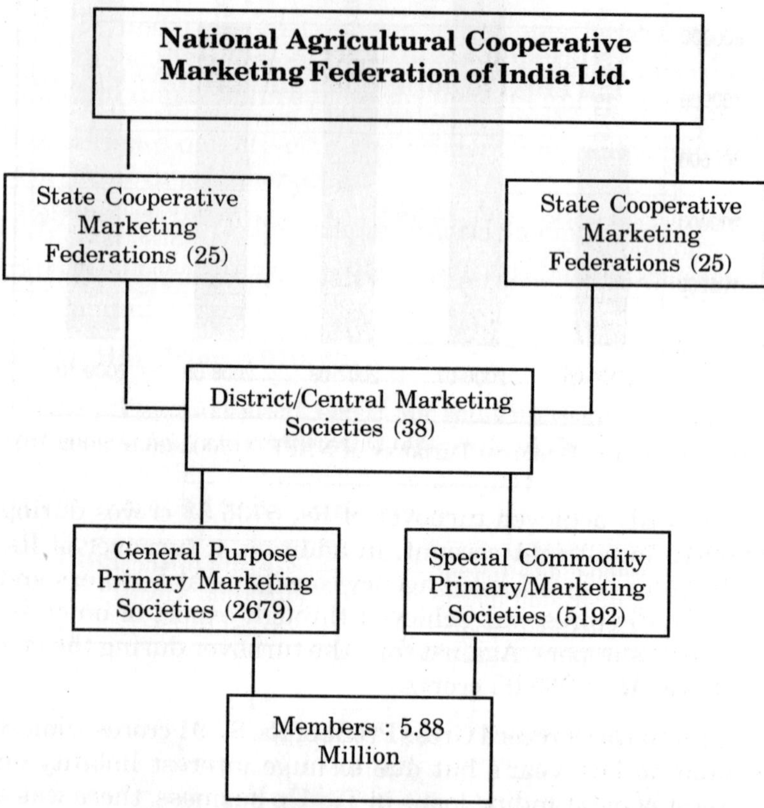

- Export of agricultural produce;
- Processing of agricultural produce;
- Coordinate with member societies in promotion of internal trade;

*NCUI, *Indian Cooperative Movement-A Statistical Profile-2009,* pp. 86-87

- Canalising agency for export of onion and nigerseed and monitoring agency for import of pulses
- Nodal agency of Government of India for price support operations;
- Production and marketing of agricultural machinery, implements and bio-fertilisers;
- Undertakes inter-state trade to stabilize consumer prices of agricultural commodities;

State Cooperative Marketing Federation

- Marketing and processing of agricultural produce;
- Supply of improved agricultural implements;
- Coordinate with member societies for marketing agricultural produce;
- Price support and market intervention operations as state agency of NAFED;
- Provide remunerative prices to farmers for their produce;

District/Central Marketing Society

- Coordinate with primary level agricultural produce societies;
- Undertake inter district trade in agricultural produce;

Primary Marketing Society

- Procurement of agricultural produce;
- Prince support and market interventions operations in association with national/state marketing federations;
- Advance loans to members in lieu of pledging their produce;

- Sale of agricultural commodities to the cooperatives and consumer organizations;
- Distribution of fertilizers and other agricultural inputs;
- Provide godown, cold storage and processing yard facilities to members;

New Areas and Future Approach

- Widen the business in marketing of food products, seeds, and fertilizers;
- Plan to set up of second plant of bio-fertilisers;
- To set up super market in Mumbai and Chennai on the lines of Nafed Bazar in Delhi;
- Exploring the possibilities to producing and marketing of hybrid seeds;
- Planning to provide market support to farmers throughout the country;
- To take up marketing of FAFED brand honey throughout the country.[4]

NOTES

1. J.B. Bhanot, "Role and Vision of Agricultural Marketing Cooperatives in New Millennium", *14th Indian Cooperative Congress Background Papers,* NCUI, p. 39.
2. *Ibid.* p. 41.
3. NAFED, A Farmers' Cooperative, business-highlight, internet papers, 5/13/2011.
4. NCUI, *Indian Cooperative Movement-A Statistical Profile-2009,* pp. 86-87.

3

National Cooperative Consumers' Federation of India Ltd. (NCCF)

The consumer cooperatives were given due importance in the national economy after Independence of the country although they were in existence since 1912.

At present there is a four-tier infrastructure of consumer cooperatives in the country, which is actively supported by the Government. There are 28290 primary societies at grass root level, 696 Wholesale/Central stores at District level, 29 State Consumer Cooperative Federations at the State level and one National apex organization i.e., National Cooperative Consumers' Federation of India Limited (NCCF).[1]

The main functions of the NCCF are (i) to act as spokesman of the consumer cooperative movement (ii) to assist and guide member institutions (iii) to provide consultancy and promotional services in various areas (iv) to promote consumer cooperatives and (v) to provide supply support to its members in particular and consumer cooperatives in general for distribution of consumer goods. The commercial operations of the NCCF are undertaken through its headquarters at New Delhi and 30 branches and sub-offices located in different parts of the country. It is also running two pulses processing units for processing of pulses.[2]

The Federation achieved sales turnover of Rs. 1322.38 crores including the business of issuing N.O.C. for export of Onion and recorded an all time high net profit of Rs. 11.17 Crores before taxation and Rs. 8.33 Crores after taxation during the year 2009-10.[3]

The Membership of the Federation was 136 as on 31.03.2010 comprising of the following:[4]

State Level consumer cooperative Federation	20
Large Sized Wholesale/Central/Primary Cooperatives	112
National Level Apex Cooperative Federations	2
Government of India	1
NCDC	1
Total	136

The paid-up share capital of the Federation as on 31.03.2010 was Rs. 13.79 crores (same as the previous year) as detail below:

	As on 31.03.2010	*As on 31.03.2009*
Cooperatives	3.03	3.03
NCDC	0.02	0.02
Government of India	10.74	10.74
Total	13.79	13.79

Against the Sales Turnover of RS. 1322 Crores for the year 2009-10, a revised work programme of Rs. 1500 Corres has been drawn up for the year 2010-11 as against original Work Programme of Rs. 1115 crores.[5]

Summary of Organisational Structure, Functions and Progress*

National Cooperative Consumers' Federation of India

NCCF

National Cooperative Consumers' Federation of India

State Cooperative Consumers' Federation

Central/District Wholesale Consumers' Cooperative Stores

Primary Consumers' Stores

Members

Main Functions

- To act as spokesman of the consumer cooperative movement;
- To assist and guide member institutions to improve their operational and managerial efficiency;
- To produce and marketing agricultural commodities such as pulses, foodgrains, sugar, tea and also manufactured items of daily use;
- Nodal Agency appointed by Government of India for import of Pulses for distribution through Fair Price Shops on subsidized rates;

*NCUI, Indian Cooperative Movement-A Statistical Profile-2009, pp. 88-89.

- To provide market intelligence to member organizations;
- Appointed by Central Government as the Nodal Agency for execution of the "SARVPRIYA" Scheme for distribution of identified selected essential consumer goods of daily use at fixed prices through the Fair Price Shops,
- Publication of quarterly magazine "Indian Consumer Cooperator" containing information and articles of consumers' interest;
- To undertake liaison with the Departments of Government of India, State Governments, NCDC, ICA, State Supplies Corporations, National Level Cooperative Organizations and the manufacturers of consumer goods;

State Consumers' Cooperative Federation

- Promote consumer cooperatives in the respective States/ UTs;
- Procure bulk quantity of consumer goods and supply to members institutions;
- Assist and guide member institutions for facilitating their working;
- Act as agent of the State Government for distribution of essential consumer items;
- Liaison with Government and other financing institutions;

Consumers' Cooperative Store:

- Protect interest of consumer;
- Supply quality essential consumer goods at reasonable rates;

- Help in maintaining price stabilization and availability of essential consumer goods;
- Liaison with State Cooperative Federations and other cooperative institutions.

Primary Agricultural Credit/Large Sized Multi Purpose Societies

- The primary agricultural credit/large sized multi purpose societies are undertaking distribution of consumer goods in addition to their other activities;
- This helps in maintaining price stabilization and availability of essential consumer goods I the rural/far flung areas.

Areas Covered and Future Approach

- NCCF proposes to diversify its activities by entering into retail trade including distribution of certified seeds and fertilizers;
- Strengthening the supply support arrangement through the consumer cooperatives by adding more items;
- Undertaking programmes for increasing consumer awareness and consumer rights as envisaged in the Consumer Protection Act.
- Arrange training programmes for the employees of the consumer cooperatives in order to improve their capabilities;
- Participation in the welfare schemes operated in the states for the upliftment of the weaker/poor section of the community;
- Expansion of import and export trade of consume goods and foodgrains.[6]

NOTES

1. T.T. Adhikari, "Progress and Problems of Consumer Cooperative Movement in India", *14th Indian Cooperative Congress,* Background Papers, NCUI, p. 283
2. *Ibid.,* p. 285
3. Internet pages NCCF-India, 05.03.2011., Directors Report.php. p. 1/7
4. *Ibid.,* p. 5/7
5. *Ibid.,* p. 6/7
6. NCUI, *Indian Cooperative Movement—A Statistical Profile-2009,* pp. 88-89

4

National Federation of State Cooperative Banks Ltd. (NAFSCOB)

The Institutional rura. cooperative credit system for agriculture comprises of short-term and long term cooperative credit institutions.

The NAFSCOB represents to the cooperative credit structure consisting of District cooperative banks and primary societies PACS, FSS & LAMPS. The federation guides and assist the affiliated members SC Bank and their affiliates in pursuing their goals and fulfillment of objectives in various spheres of activities.

The short-term cooperative credit structure includes 31 State Cooperative Banks (SCBs) with 986 branches, 372 District Central Cooperative Banks (DCCBs) with 13151 branches and 93634 Primary Agricultural Credit Society (PACS) in the country.[1]

The statistical details of primary agriculture credit societies (PACS), district central cooperative banks (DCCBS) and state cooperative banks (SCBs) as the end of March 2008 are as follows:

Primary Societies (PACS, FSS & LAMPS)			*District Central Cooperative Banks (DCCBs)*	
1. Societies (Nos.)	97224	1.	DCCBs (Nos.)	371
2. Branches (Nos.)	NIL	2.	Branches	12928
3. Membership	125792	3.	Membership	3265
4. Owned Funds	1103884	4.	Owned Funds	2060325
5. Deposits	2348407	5.	Deposits	9208136
6. Borrowings	4371449	6.	Borrowings	2794060
7. Loans & Adv.	4961275	7.	Loans &Adv.	7670381
8. Loans Outs.	5862015	8.	Loans Outs.	8546075
9. Overdues to demand	29.11%	9.	Overdues to demand	32.93%
10. Employees (Nos.)	229007	10.	Employees (Nos.)	183536
11. Borrowers (Nos.)	47910			

State Cooperative Banks	
1. SCBs (Nos.)	31
2. Branches	938
3. Membership	149
4. Owned Funds	958158
5. Deposits	4846961
6. Borrowings	2215024
7. Loans &Adv.	4706898
8. Loans Outs.	4667581
9. Overdues to demand	13.27%
10. Employees (Nos.)	14748

It provides an affective focum for the member banks. During 2008-09 the federation convened four meetings to review performance and functioning of the short-term credit structure and issues of concern. Also a memorandum was submitted to the Government of India on behalf of the short term credit cooperative institutions.

The Forty Fifth Annual General Body Meeting of the NAFSCOB was held in September 2008 at Bhubaneshwar. The Board of Directors of NAFSCOM convened meetings four times between April 01, 2008 to March 31, 2009 to review the performance and functioning of the short term cooperative credit structure as well as to discuss and deliberate on various issues of concern to the short term cooperative credit structure and to find solutions to the problem of short term cooperative credit structure. The Executive Committee of NAFSCOB met six times during the year.[2] It has submitted a memorandum on pertient issues to the Government of India.

Summary of Organisational Structure, Functions and Progress*

National Federation of State Cooperative Banks NAFSCOB

Agricultural Credit Cooperatives Production Credit

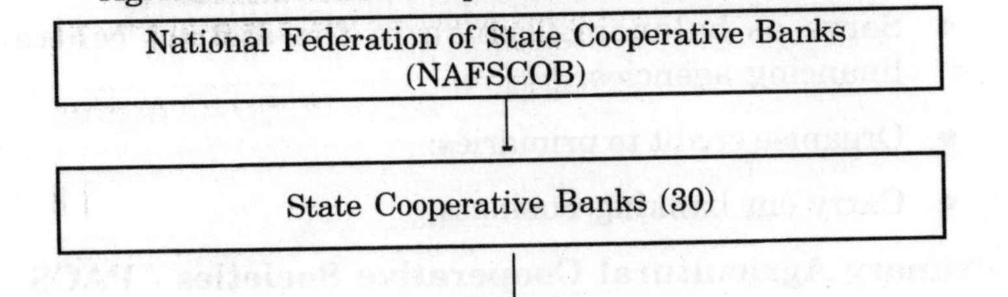

*NCUI, Indian Cooperative Movement—A Statistical Profile 2009, pp.90-91.

Main Functions

National Federation of State Cooperative Banks

- Provides a common forum to the member banks;
- Promote and protects the interests of the member banks;
- Co-ordinates and liaison with Government of India, Reserve bank of India, National Bank and others;
- Provides research and consultancy inputs to the member banks;
- Organises conferences/seminars/workshops/meetings;

State Cooperative Banks

- Serve as balancing centre in the states;
- Organise provision of credit for credit worthy farmers;
- Carry out banking business;
- Leader of the Cooperatives in the states;

District Central Cooperative Banks

- Serve as balancing centre in the district central financing agencies;
- Organise credit to primaries;
- Carry out banking business;

Primary Agricultural Cooperative Societies / PACS

- Assessment of credit needs;
- Disbursement of credit to members;
- Recovery of credit;
- Promote the economic interest of the members;

Future Approach

- NAFSCOB will continue to ensure that effective common forum is provided for the SCBs for discussing policy issues pertaining to credit banking, deposits banking and general banking and also allied issues to members SCBs.

- NAFSCOB will continue to strive for acquiring freedom of functional autonomy to their affiliates;
- NAFSCOB will continue to work towards maintaining and restoring the principles of democracy in the management of cooperative credit institutions;
- To develop and establish sound information network among the Member Banks,

New Areas

- Professionaliation;
- Human Resource Development and Management;
- Prudent banking and investment Policies;
- Restructing and revitalization measures.[3]

NOTES

1. NCUI, "Brief Report of National Level Cooperative Organizations", *Annual Report, 2009-10,* p. 73.
2. NCUI, *Annual Report 2008-09,* p. 88.
3. NCUI, *Indian Cooperative Movement—A Statistical Profile 2009,* pp. 90-91.

5

National Cooperative Agriculture and Rural Development Banks (NCARDB)

The long-term credit structure comprises of Agriculture and Rural Development Banks (ARDBs) at the State level operating through their branches in some states and through affiliated Primary Agricultural Development Banks in others. Agriculture and Rural Development Banks are specialized term lending institutions in cooperative sector catering mainly to the investment credit needs of agriculture and rural sectors. Entire advances of Agriculture and Rural Development Banks are going for capital formation in rural areas. ARDBs finance investment credit projects for a wide range of activities covering agriculture and allied sectors, rural non-farm sector consisting of agricultural processing, marketing and transportation, small scale and rural industries and rural housing.[1]

The birth place of L.M. Banking is Silesia a town in Germany where the first Bank was established in 1769. The real beginning of land mortgage banking in India was made in 1929 in Madras. To facilitate the working of land mortgage banks, the Madras Cooperative Land Mortgage Banks Act was passed in 1934 which has been suitably amended from time to time.[2]

The ARDBs were established as Land Mortgage Banks with the sole objective of relieving the farmers of their heavy burden of debts taken from private money lenders at exorbitantly high rate of interest. The Land Mortgage Banks had undergone organizational, conceptual and attitudinal changes time and again to keep pace with the changing political and socio economic environment and governmental policies. While these banks functioned as Land Mortgage Banks till 1955, they took up the task of providing long term credit for productive purposes in the farm sector in the context of planned economic development envisaged under the development planning in India and in the process converted themselves in to Land Development Banks. Later on in 1980s, these banks broad-based their operations and started extending investing credit for rural development, including non-land based and non-agricultural activities too. The emergence of present day Agriculture and Rural Development Banks can thus be traced to their positive response to the changing credit needs of rural sector over the years.[3]

The **Federation** came into existence in 1960 and is administered under the Multi State Cooperative Societies, 2002. Its main function is to keep liaison with NABARD and other State National Level agencies. The Planning Research and Development cell is active in arranging researches, conducting conferences and seminars. Also it takes interests in studying rural credit system and its related problems.

Summary of Organisational Structure, Functions and Progress*

Agricultural Credit Cooperatives Investment Credit

National Cooperative Agriculture and Rural Development Banks' Federation Ltd.

State Coop. Agril/Rural Development Banks (SCARDBs) (19)

Regional/Division/District Offices (225)

Primary Coop. Agrl. & Rural Development Banks (PCARDBs) (684)
Branches of State Co-op. Agr. & Rural Development Banks (775)
and Branches of PCARDBs/Sub-Branches of SCARDBs (1062)

Borrowing & Non Borrowing Members : 14.37 Million

Main Functions

National Cooperative Agriculture and Rural Development Bank's Federation Ltd.

- Coordinating the lending and resource mobilization programmes of SCARDBs at national level;
- Advocacy, spokesmanship and lobbying on behalf of member banks;
- Publications, guidance and consultancy services on HRD, financial management and investment of funds etc. along with conducting seminars and workshops;

*NCUI, Indian Cooperative Movement—A Statistical Profile 2009, pp. 92-93

- Business development services to member banks;
- Liaison with Govt. of India, Planning Commission, RBI, NABARD, NHB, nationalized banks, commercial banks, cooperative banks and other concerned on matters relating to long term credit.
- Establishing and foresting relations with international organizations/agencies and national level cooperatives abroad.

State Cooperative Agriculture and Rural Development Banks

- Purveyance of investment credit directly/through affiliated primary banks;
- Formulation of long term investment policies and perspective credit plans with yearly review and mobilizing resources for implementing such credit programmes through debentures, loans, deposits etc.
- Providing technical support and guidance to farmers through primaries;
- Liaison with Government, NABARD, NCARDBF, NHB, nationalized banks and other institutions;

District/Regional/Divisional Offices

- Investment credit to members for agriculture and rural sector;
- Extension services to farmers;
- Monitoring of loans;
- Recovery of loans;

Future Approach

- To pursue vigorously with Central and State Governments for reviving LTCCS involving recapitalization, legal and institutional reforms;

- To pursue with RBI/Government for conversion of ARDBs into full-fledged banks;
- To coordinate and work with NABARD for institutional reforms in the LTCCS;
- To work for restoration and strengthening democratic set up in cooperative investment credit institutions;
- To promote state level investment credit Institutions in those states where such institutions do not exist;
- To develop and establish sound information network among the member banks;

New Areas

- Identify emerging opportunities for business development by member banks;
- Capacity building of ARDB staff in diversified business portfolios;
- Helping member banks to become resource based and self reliant;
- Enhanced support to member banks for improving loan recovery.[4]

NOTES

1. K. K. Ravindran, "Revitalisation of Cooperative Long Term Credit Structure", *14th Indian Cooperative Congress, Background papers,* NCUI, p. 77.
2. Sami uddin & Mahfoozur Rahman, *Cooperative Sector in India,* S. Chand & Company, 1983, p. 142-143.
3. K. K. Ravindran, *Op.cit.,* p. 77.
4. NCUI, *Indian Cooperative Movement—A Statistical Profile 2009,* pp. 92-93.

6

Indian Farmers Fertilisers Cooperative Limited (IFFCO)

India is predominantly an agricultural country. The agricultural sector of the economy needs more care as the Industrial development depends upon agricultural output. The government is taking care of the problem and giving more attention to the development of fertilizers as it has a direct bearing on economic growth. It is estimated that about 50% increase in agricultural production could be attributed to fertilizer usage. Looking into the need the first manufacturing unit of Single Super Phosphate (SSP) was set up in Ranjpet near Chennai with an annual capacity of 6000 MT. The Fertilizer and Chemicals Travancore of India Ltd. (FACT) at Cochin in Kerala and the Fertilizers Corporation of India (FCI) in Sindri in Bihar were the first large sized-fertilizer plants set up in the forties and fifties with a view to establish an industrial base to achieve self-sufficiency in foogdrains. Before 1967, the cooperatives were entirely dependent on private and public sector manufacturers for their requirements of fertilizers for distribution. The suppliers used to exploit the situation to their advantage by not making timely supplies. This made cooperatives think of having their own manufacturing facilities.[1]

Indian Farmers Fertiliser Cooperative Ltd. (IFFCO) was formed at the initiative of cooperative institutions of India and the Cooperative League of USA now know as NCBI and registered as a Cooperative Society on November 3, 1967 under the Multi-Unit Cooperative Societies Act, 1942.[2]

The Fertiliser Industry in India has been playing a pivotal role in making available the adequate quantities of plant nutrients for achieving not only the goal of self-sufficiency in food grains production but also to have a rapid growth of agriculture.[3]

Indian cooperatives were working as an arm of the Government upto late 70's and virtually had the monopoly of fertiliser distribution by controlling more than 70 percent of the total fertiliser sales in the country. However, on the recommendations of Sivaraman Committee, private trade also entered the fertilsier field. The private trade soon made a recognizable place in Public/Private sector fertiliser units who hitherto were giving preference to cooperatives in fertiliser supplies. Lack of production facilities of their own was proving to be a major constraint in growth of cooperatives for effectively serving the members. Cooperatives, were therefore, looking for an assured and dependable source of supply of fertilizers to meet their requirement.[4]

Presently there are two fertiliser cooperatives IFFCO and KRIBHCO in the field of production and marketing of fertilizers. However, IFFCO is fully owned by member cooperatives. The total production capacity of IFFCO is 37 lakh MTPA of Urea and 22 lakh MTPA of NPK/DAP and that of KRIBHCO is 17 lakh MTPA of Urea.[5]

With the enactment of the Multi State Cooperative Societies Act 2002, IFFCO was deemed to be registered as a

hest Sale of Fertilisers	118.27 Lakh MT (Previous Best 112.58 Lakh MT in 2008-09)
hest Sale of Urea	63.35 Lakh MT (Previous Best 58.69 Lakh MT in 2008-09)
hest Sale of NPK/DAP/NP	54.29 Lakh MT (Previous Best 53.89 Lakh MT in 2008-09)
fit Before Tax	Rs. 567.28 Crore (Best PBT Rs. 807.09 Crore in 2002-03)
fit After Tax	Rs. 401.10 Crore (Best PAT Rs. 557.2 crore in 2002-03)
al Turnover	Rs. 16,809 crore (Previous Best Rs. 32,933 crore in 2008-09)
nt Productivity	1,608 MT per employee (Previous Best 1,669 MT in 2005-06)
ghest Marketing Productivity	7,885 MT per employee (Previous Best 7,397 MT in 2008-09)

The progress made by cooperatives in the field of fertilizers oduction has been immense. Now the cooperatives cover proximately 99% of India's villages, 67% of the total rural pulation. They also account for about 45% of the total riculture credit disbursed and 36% of the total quantity of tilsiers distributed in the country. IFFCO is a major operative in the production of fertilizer in India, its share counts for around 20% in total production of N and 24% P produced in the country.

Multi-state Cooperative Society under the M this has provided functional autonomy to the play a bigger role in their development. Ur 2002 The role of the registrar of the cooperati been redefined as a facilitator. The new reduced the role of the Government and enco making by the professionals. The enactment also created a favourable legislative environ catalyst towards strengthening the cooperat The equity contribution of GOI was 70% in promulgation of Multi State Cooperative Soc and the recognition of the need of a Nati cooperative to phase out the Governmen cooperatives, the cooperatives actively support per cent shareholding in IFFCO, thereby ma cooperative in true sense.[6]

IFFCO aims to augment the increment farmers by helping them to increase their cro through balanced use of energy efficient fertili the environmental health; and to make cooper economically and democratically strong for pr services to the farming community to ensure a rural India.[7]

The performance highlight for 2009-10 are

Highest Production of Fertilisers	81.98 Lakh Best 71.68 La 09)
Highest Production of Urea	43.24 Lakh Best 40.68 La 09)
Production of NPK/DAP/NP	38.74 Lakh Best 112.58 2008-09)

Hi Hi Hi Pr Pr To Pl H

pr ap p ag fe c a fo

Table 5.1 indicates All India Share of IFFCO from 2007-08 to 2009-10.

		2007-08	*2008-09*	*2009-10*
N	All India Production	10902	10900	11914
	Capacity utilization	89%	89%	97%
	IFFCO Production	2236	2329	2585
	Capacity Utilization (revamped Capacity w.e.f. 2008-09)	94%	94%	98%
	IFFCO Share	**21%**	**21%**	**22%**
P2O5	All India Production	3714	3417	4349
	Capacity Utilisation	63%	58%	74%
	IFFCO Production	994	918	1194
	Capacity Utilization	58%	53%	70%
	IFFCO share	**27%**	**27%**	**28%**

The major problems being faced by the cooperatives have been in respect of finding reasonable market for their produce, problems concerning their structure needing internal sectoral adjustments. Some areas of concern as highlighted by Dr. Awasthi are given below:[9]

a. The present federal structure does not provide strength to IFFCO because of weakness of the organizational structure of cooperatives.

b. The cooperatives at the primary level with their limited resources are not able to meet the challenges posed by the private players.

c. Because of involvement of may parties in the cooperative distribution channel the primary level societies do not get a fair share resulting their failure.

d. Participation of the Government in the functioning of these societies has led to the erosion of autonomy in their working.

e. The societies also suffer because of poor infrastructural facilities including roads, godowns and storage facilities.

f. Because of their poor recovery the cooperatives are not developing their business group over members.

g. Poor recovery of crop loans/heavy overdues from members have also resulted in losses to the cooperative societies at the primary level. Agri input prices have risen and so have the business risks associated with agriculture but there has been no proportionate increase in the Cooperative Credit Component available to the farmers and sale prices of agriculture produce.

Inspite of all this the fertilizer cooperatives have played an important role in achieving self sufficiency in foodgrains production. The government has also provided logistics support which led to its growth.

Summary of Organisational Structure, Functions and Progress*

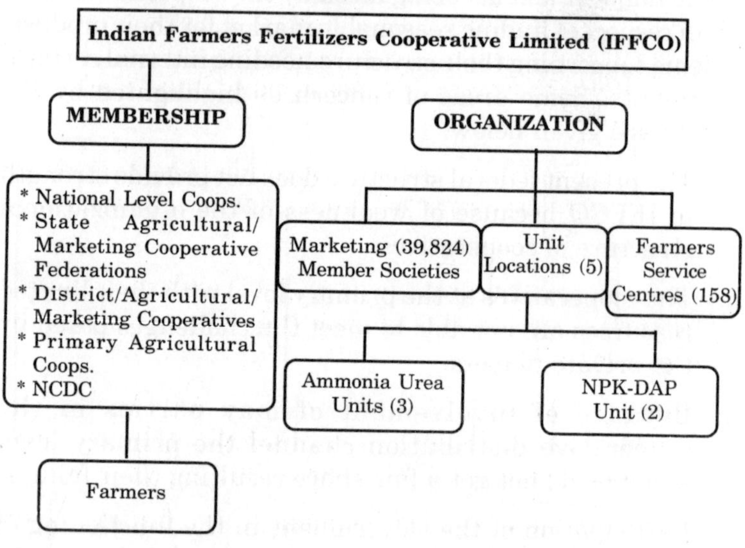

*NCUI, Indian Cooperative Movement—A Statistical Profile-2009, pp.94-95.

Main Functions

- Augmenting Fertiliser Production;
- Ensure timely availability of fertilizers and other agro-inputs at the farmer's door-steps;
- Strengthening fertiliser cooperative distribution system;
- Cooperative development programmes (2008-09);
- Cooperative Rural Development Trust (CORDET) providing practical training to farmers to improve their skills. During the year 216 training programmes were organized.
- 195 Storage-Cum-Community Centres have been set up till date
- Rural and Agriculture Development Programmes
- Farmers Education and Training Programmes
- Village Adoption programmes (439 villages were adopted during 2008-09)
- Balanced Fertilisation Programmes
- Promotional programmes : Sale Point Personnel Training, Field Day,
- Production and Soil Testing
- IFFCO Kisan Sewa Trust to provide relief and rehabilitation to victims of national calamities, provide welfare and critical medical attention for needy, poor farmers.
- Cooperative Development Fund to provide financial assistance and encourage member cooperative societies to under take efforts towards their betterment.

New Areas

- Diversification into Insurance Sector through IFFCO Tokio General Insurance Company Limited (ITGI).

- IFFCO is playing an important role in Rural Telecom Sector through IFFCO Kisan Sanchar Limited (IKSL).
- Diversification into Power Sector by incorporating Joint Venture Company "IFFCO Chhatisgarh Power Limited" to set up a 1320 MW Coal-based Mega Power Plant in Chhattisgarh.
- IFFCO has been a major promoter of National Commodity and Derivative Exchange Limited (NCDEX) and National Collateral Management Services Limited (NCMSL) the front runners in providing avenues for commodity trading and collateral management services to the Indian farmers.
- IFFCO Kisan Bazar Limite (IKBL) is incorporated for undertaking business in agri-inputs an consumer goods for the benefit of farmers and cooperatives.
- IFFCO is setting up a multi-product "IFFCO Kisan SEZ" at Nellore (A.P.) with primary focus on food processing and agri-based Industries.
- IFFCO has promoted "Indian Farm Forestry and Development Cooperative Limited (IFFDC)" a multi state cooperative society working towards development of wasteland and enhancement of socio-economic status of rural poor.
- Establishment of "IFFCO Foundation" for cooperative, social, cultural and human resource development.

Future Approach – Vision 2010

- Installation of Ammonia/Urea plants including acquisition of fertiliser units;
- Backward integration to meet feedstock requirements such as phosphoric and acid etc.
- Generation of power;

- Production and marketing of micro-nutrients, seeds, bio-fertilises, pesticides etc.
- Value addition to agri-products and marketing;
- Information Technology and IT enabled services;
- Establishments of retail chain in urban and semi-urban locations;
- Diversification into new growth areas such as mobile telephony and communication technology in the rural areas.
- Under "VISION 2010", the Society has targeted to achieve an annual turnover of Rs. 15,000 crores. This landmark has since been achieved, with the turnover for the year 2008-09 amounting to Rs. 32,933 crores.[10]

NOTES

1. U.S. Awasthi, "Role and Vision of Fertiliser Cooperatives in New Millennium", 14th Indian Cooperative Congress, *Background Papers*, NCUI, New Delhi, p. 26.
2. *Ibid.*
3. *Ibid.*
4. *Ibid.*
5. *Ibid.*
6. *Ibid.*
7. *Ibid.*
8. *Ibid.*
9. NCUI, Awasthi "Reforms Introduction Vision of Fertilizer Cooperatives for Autonomous and Competitive Functioning" 15th Indian Cooperative Congress, *Background Papers,* 2008, NCUI, p. 33.
10. NCUI, *Indian Cooperative Movement—A Statistical Profile–2009*, pp. 94-95.

7

Krishak Bharati Cooperative Ltd. (KRIBHCO)

The Indian Farmers Fertiliser Cooperative Limited (IFFCO) was formed during 1967 as an experiment in a sophisticated field which eventually blossomed to occupy a place of pride in the Indian Fertiliser Industry. The success of IFFCO encouraged the cooperators to venture into one of the largest fertiliser projects in the world i.e., Krishak Bharti Cooperative Limited (KRIBHCO) which was registered on 17th April, 1980 to implement a giant Ammonia/Urea Complex at Hazira in Gujarat State. KRIBHCO is a national level multi-state cooperative society jointly promoted by government of India, IFFCO and Cooperative Societies from all over the country. Installed capacity of the complex is 14.52 lakh tones per annum.[1]

The important objectives of the society are to promote the economic interest of its members by undertaking manufacture of fertilizers and allied products with maximum efficiency; rendering services to the farmers through the cooperative channel; strengthening the cooperatives; working as a catalyst for uplifting the socio-economic status of the farmers and undertaking such other activities which are conducive to the development of agriculture and rural development.[2]

Keeping in view of the limited scope for expansion in the fartiliser sector coupled with the changed economic scenario in the country following liberalization measures being taken by the Central Government, the object clause was expanded to make provision for diversification of activities of KRIBHCO. Accordingly, some more areas like production of agricultural items including mushroom, food processing industries, agro-based industries, aquaculture, forestry and certain other industries of national importance have been added.

Krishak Bharti Cooperative Limited (KRIBHCO) started its commercial production in March, 1986. Since inception, its plants have been operating at a very high level of capacity utilization i.e., around 100-110% of its installed capacity which has been upgraded to 17.06 lakh MTs Urea per annum. The operation of plants at such a high level has been possible by regular and timely maintenance, modernizing the plants with the new/latest technology and above all the professional team of engineers. The unique feature of the plant is production of urea at the minimum cost in fertilsier sector.[3]

Production Performance

KRIBCO has entered the 24th year of commercial operation during 2009-10. Society's fertilizer plant at Hazira, Surat maintained its good performance during the year and achieved its production target. The Society produced 17.80 Lakh MT of Urea and 11.10 Lakh MT of Ammonia which corresponds to capacity utilization of 102.94% and 110.65% respectively. The cumulative Urea and Ammonia production since inception crossed 39 million MT and 24 million MT respectively as on March 31, 2010. The Society's Plant dispatched 17.76 lakh MT of Urea to various destinations throughout the country during the year. The Society also produced 3556.7 thousand Nm' Argon.[4]

Marketing is the backbone of any commercial organization. KRIBHCO has got the trained professional manpower who are basically either agriculture or management graduates for marketing of its products. KRIBHCO is primarily involved in marketing of Urea and other agro-inputs including DAP which are key inputs for higher agricultural production and profitability of farmers. For the benefit of majority of the farmers, KRIBHCO is presently marketing in all major states. The marketing operations are managed by field force positioned at district/ area and state levels. Supplies of products, required by the farmers, are provided in adequate quantity at right time and at right place. Though KRIBHCO's marketing started with a severe competition in the market during 1986-87/88, the professional field force of KRIBHCO has been able to excel in marketing inspite of several odds like drought condition, glut situation etc. and KRIBHCO has always been able to sell its products at the minimum cost and inventory with early realization of sales proceeds.[5]

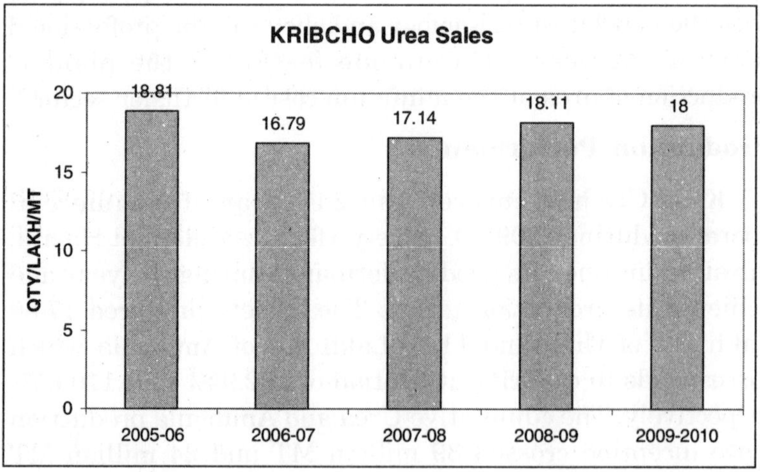

Ref. p. 17 KRIBCO

The society has established strong relationship with faming community through extensive network of marketing and extension experts, spread over in most of the major states. This has helped the society to create strong Brand Image amongst the farmers.

Marketing channel of KRIBHCO includes Cooperative Apex Federations, Institutional Agencies and Grass Root Level Societies. The direct supplies to Primary Agricultural Cooperative Society (PACS) help these societies immensely as the timely supplies enable them to increase fertiliser consumption and productivity as well as to draw maximum financial benefits.[6]

Strategy for Fertiliser Marketing Development

The approach towards problems faced by the cooperative in marketing of fertilizers should be to develop the cooperative infrastructure at the grass-root level and to provide necessary funds to enable them to play a large and effective role. At the same time rational planning for sharing of the distribution margins, keeping in view the role performed at each level, has to be worked out so as to provide an incentive to the retail cooperatives in this activity. Some of the specific measures which need to be taken-up by the cooperative organizations are indicated below to strengthen the cooperatives particularly in relation to fertiliser marketing:

1. Comprehensive development of primary agricultural credit societies to function as multi-purpose viable units.
2. Realignment of policies and procedures of cooperatives to expand the flow of credit and ensure supply of inputs and services, particularly to the weaker sections.
3. Promoting professional management and strengthening training facilities of cooperative personnel.
4. Enhancing cash credit limit of the primary level societies at concessional rates.

5. To provide adequate margin money to primary level societies.
6. Development of infrastructure facilities at the primary level societies.
7. Construction of additional storage capacity with the primary level societies.
8. To undertake distribution of not only fertilizers but the entire gamut of agro-inputs like seeds, pesticides and implements etc., to the farmers under one roof.
9. Proper incentive to the cooperatives salesmen for achieving higher sales.
10. Autonomy to the societies in decision making.
11. Development of loyalty to the cooperative fertilsier manufacturers.[7]

Production Plan 2010-2011

The production plant target for the Financial year 2010-2011 is 17.53 lakh MT of Urea and 10.55 lakh MT of Ammonia, which corresponds to a capacity utilization of 101.4% and 105.2% respectively.[8]

Kribhco Ammonia and Urea Capacity Utilization

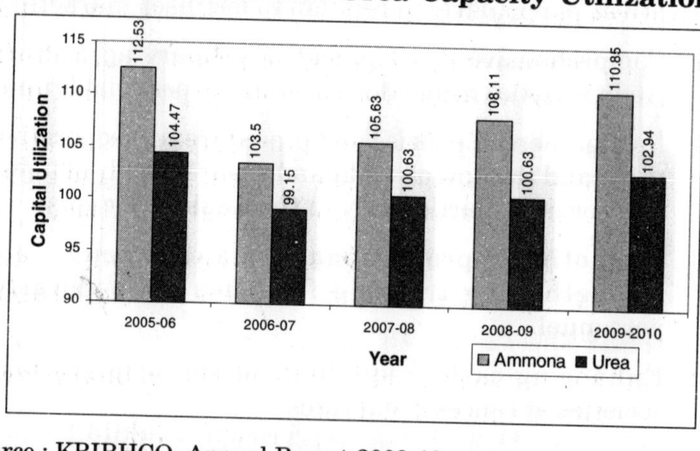

Source : KRIBHCO, Annual Report 2009-10, p. 14

Financial Performance

The KRIBHCO has achieved excellent financial results for the Financial year 2009-2010. The society has posted pre-tax profit of Rs. 252.77 crore during the year and profit after tax is Rs. 228.17 crore. The net worth of the society has increased from Rs. 2,549.41 crore to Rs. 2697.12 crores as on March 31, 2010. The financial results of the society for the year are summarized in table 6.1:[9]

Table 6.1

	2009-10	*2008-2009*
Sales Turnover including subsidies	2597.07	2,559.12
Other Revenue	304.78	409.75
Increase (Decrease) in Stock	-38.19	-58.90
Income	2663.66	2,909.97
Profit before Tax	252.77	269.34
Provision for Taxation (Net)	24.60	19.21
Profit after Tax	228.17	250.13

Seed Multiplication Programme and Marketing of Hybrid

Seed

Seed is the basic and most critical input for sustainable agriculture. The response of all other inputs depends on quality of seeds to large extent. It is estimated that the contribution of quality seed alone to the total production is about 20-255 depending upon the crop and it can be further raised to 45% with efficient Management of other inputs.[10]

Considering the high potential of Hybrid seed to improve plant vigor and increased yield, the society plans to make Hybrid Seed of major crops i.e., Cotton Paddy and Maize during 2010-11. During 2009-2010, the Society sold 2.22 lakh qts. Of certified seed of various crops and varieties which contribute 1.02% in the national seed availability. The society plans to produce 3.45 lakh qts. Of seed during 2010-2011.

Seed Production and Sales

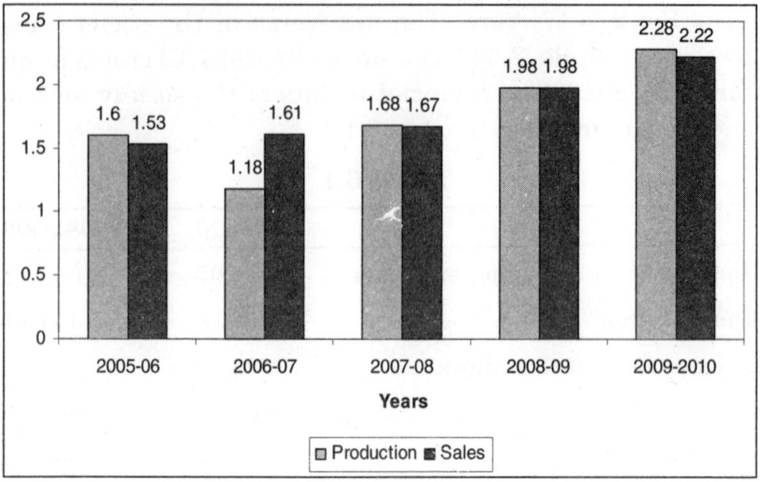

Source : KRIBCHO, p. 19

In a way KRIBHCO is committed to inclusive growth and believes in improving the quality of life of the farmers. The society has been taking concrete action by focusing primarily on the upliftment of communities in health, family welfare, education, environment protection, institution building etc.[11]

Main Function

- Production of Ammonia, Urea, Argo and Bio-Fartilisers.
- Making available fertilizers, seeds, bio-fartilisers to farmers at door-steps.
- Education and training of farmers;
- Transfers of technology for modern farming;
- Organize farmer services programme such as farmer meetings, kisan meals, field demonstrations, field days,

Summary of Organisational Structure, Functions and Progress

Krishak Bharati Cooperative Ltd. (KRIBHCO)

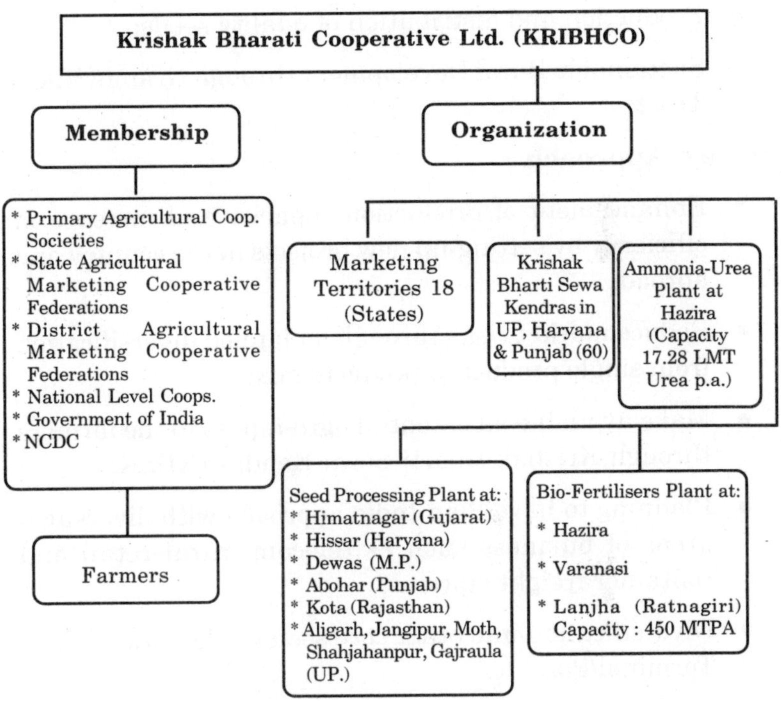

cooperative conferences, group discussions, special campaigns etc. (2500 programmes across the country benefiting 11.69 lakh farmers).

- Kribhco Krishi Paramarsh Kendra at Noida for free consultancy on farm related issues;
- Advanced soil testing laboratory at Noida for free consultancy on farm related issues;

- Advanced soil testing laboratory at Noida for free soil nutrients and irrigation water testing;
- Free insurance coverage for farmers under "Kisan Aapada Nivaran Bima Yojna";
- Strengthening of cooperative system;
- Production and distribution of quality seeds;
- Sustainable Rural Development through Gramin Vikas Trust.

Future Approach

- Enhancement of production capacity and increase in efficiency by setting-up new projects in the country and abroad;
- Reduce market risks through a planned diversification from single product to products mix;
- Make available all essential agro-inputs to the farmers through Krishak Bharti Sewa Kendra (KBSK)
- Planning to have Plan India approach with diversified areas of business such as telecom, rural retail and container freight stations;
- Diversification into other core sectors like Power, LNG Terminal/Port etc.[12]

NOTES

1. KRIBHCO, "Progress and Strategies for Fertilsier Cooperative Development"14th Indian Cooperative Congress, *Background Papers,* NCUI, New Delhi, p. 344.
2. *Ibid.,* pp. 344-345.
3. *Ibid.,* p. 345.
4. KRIBHCO, *30th Annual Report 2009-10,* p. 13.
5. KRIBHCO, *Op.cit.,* p. 345.
6. KRIBHCO, *30th Annual Report 2009-10,* p. 17.

7. KRIBHCO, *Op.cit.*, p. 347.

8. KRIBHCO, *30th Annual Report 2009-10,* p.14.

9. *Ibid.*, p. 12.

10. *Ibid.*, p. 19.

11. *Ibid.*, p. 25.

12. *Indian Cooperative Movement–A Statistical Profile-2009,* pp. 96-97.

8

Tribal Cooperative Marketing Development Federationof India Ltd. (TRIFED)

The cooperatives were introduced in the tribal areas to ameliorate the socio economic conditions of the tribal people and protect them from the exploitation of money lenders, contractors and middlemen in the marketing of minor forest produces.

The main three sources of Income for tribals are:

1. Collection of Minor Forest Produces;
2. Agriculture (cultivation) and related activities; and
3. Employment as casual labourers.[1]

The tribals draw sustenance and income including their requirements for food, fodder, fruits, and medicine from the Non Wood Forest Produce (NWFP) of the forest.

The commercial importance of NWFPs can be gauged from the fact that NWFPs are estimated to generate Rs. Three billion annually and 70% of all employment in the Indian Forestry sector.

The magnitude of the dependence of the tribals on NWFPs of the natural forests, and the need to enlist their participation in the development, growth and marketing of NWFPs has been recognized by the Government and was emphasized in the National Forest Policy Statement of 1988.[2]

In order to cater to the credit and marketing needs of the tribals, LAMPS were organized since 1974 as an instrument of tribal development during the sixth plan to provide the major facilities. They were organized either by converting the PACS, or by organizing new LAMPS at the block level so as to cover at least 10000 acres of agricultural land and an annual short-term credit potential of Rs. 51 lakhs.

In the second tier system State Tribal Development Corporations (STDs) were created at the state level to help these LAMPS in procurement of Minor Forest Produces and at the national level *Tribal Cooperative Marketing Development Federation of India Ltd. (TRIFED)* was established in 1987 to help the STDCs and LAMPS in the marketing of tribal produces.[3]

The national level apex cooperative, TRIFED, which in its existence of more than two decade has achieved a high market turn over and has managed to place some of the NWFPs in the export list of the country and with the backing of the Central Government plays a role in Price Support operations with regard to NWFPs. Because, of the absence of a viable network of cooperative societies or even state run agencies at the state or district level and more so, at the village level in tribal dominated states it is difficult for the TRIFED to work effectively. Nationalisation and the system of allocating NWFPs to the highest bidder, have also restricted the TRIFED's access to these NWFPs market. However, TRIFED has managed to make an impact in the NWFPs marketing through interventions in association with some of the more active cooperatives.

Designating TRIFED as the implementing agency for collection of MFPs (a scheme needs to be formulated) and for Agricultural Produces, the scheme exists but needs the extension to include TRIFED as procuring agency from Tribal areas, as TRIFED has the expertise of collection of Agricultural Produces all over India since a decade.[4]

Summary of Organisational Structure, Functions and Progress*

Tribal Cooperative Marketing Development Federation of India Limited (TRIFED)

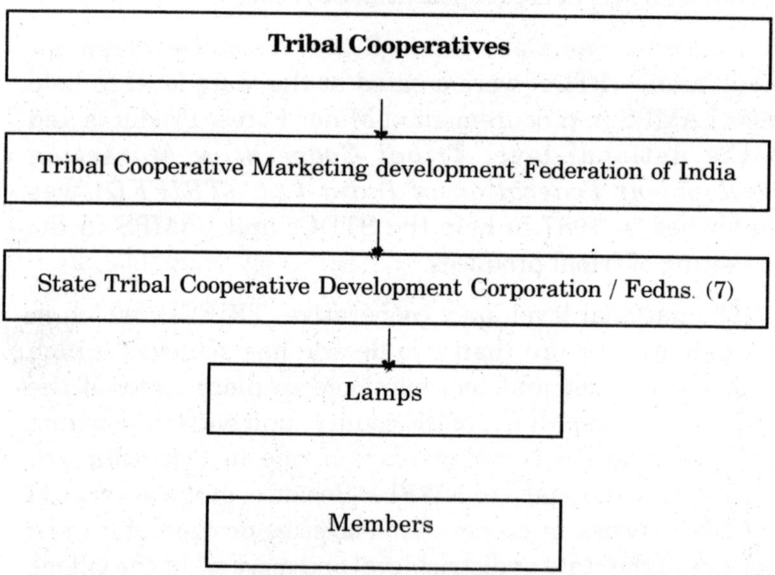

National Level Cooperative Federation responsible for marketing development of tribal produce and handicrafts Established in 1987.

*NCUI, Indian Cooperative Movement—A Statistical Profile-2009, pp. 98-99.

The main objective of Tribal Cooperative Marketing Development Federation of India Ltd. (TRIFED) shall be to serve the interests of its members in more than one state for the social and economic betterment of its members by conducting its affairs in professional, democratic and autonomous manner through self help and mutual cooperation for undertaking marketing development of the tribal products.

Main Functions

- To facilitate, coordinate and promote the marketing of the tribal products by its members.
- To undertake/promote on behalf of its members/ institutions or the government or government organizations, inter-state and international marketing of tribal products.
- To act as agency for canalization of export and import and facilitate, wherever necessary inter-state trade of tribal products under any scheme formulated by government of India or any other state agencies.
- To develop market intelligence related to supply, demand, price trends, supply/market chain, value addition and processing facilities, product quality specifications, products applications, market trends, buyers for the tribal products and disseminate the information to the members as well as planners, researchers and associate organizations and business circles etc.
- To assists in capability and capacity building of the members relating to the marketing development of the tribal products.
- To expand and extend the markets for tribal products through marketing development and promotion programmes.

- To assist in the development of new products through product development, product innovation, products designs, new product applications and special R & D drives for tribal products;
- To strive for development of fair trade mechanism for tribal products and marketing thereof.
- To develop quality specifications and quality preservations systems for tribal products in collaboration with all related organizations/departments/institutions.
- To initiate and promote creation of technologies and infrastructure for basic value addition on the tribal products;
- To formalize and organize the market for tribal products by bringing all functionaries together with members, buyers, facilitator, processors and sellers to harness global synergy advantages.
- To identify items of minor forest produce (MFP) in different states to be brought under the ambit of the cooperative marketing and make recommendations for fixation of minimum prices of such MFP in the tribal areas by each State.
- To organize seminar, workshops, conferences, exhibitions, trade-fairs and such other activities within the country and abroad to further the objectives of TRIFED.
- To promote setting up of units of production value addition of tribal products.

State Tribal Cooperative Development Corporations/ Federations

- Collection of minor forest produce through LAMPS

Future Approach

- Undertaking livelihood generation projects in tribal areas for marketing development of tribal products;
- Sectoral approach of cluster development in tribal areas on entrepreneurship model for economic development of tribals.
- Capacity and capability building of members as well as tribals in marketing development of tribal products.
- Developing markets through brand building of tribal products for national as well as international markets.
- Greater emphasis on value addition at primary level to create employment opportunities in tribals areas, promotion of interstate and international trade.
- Promoting marketing infrastructure facilities and qualities for tribal/forest products.

New Areas

- Marketing research and studies for selected tribals products.
- R & D for tribals products;
- Marketing of herbal medicines and cosmetics.[5]

NOTES

1. TRIFED "Tribal Cooperatives-Role and Vision in New Millennium, Progress, Problems and Trends, 14th Indian Cooperative Congress *Background Papers,* Sept. 2001, NCUI, p. 337.
2. A.K. Kaul, "Impact of Marketing Intervention on the Tribal Economy", *14th Indian Cooperative Congress Souvenir, September, 2001,* NCUI, p. 113.
3. TRIFED "Tribal Cooperatives-Role and Vision in New Millennium, Progress, Problems and Trends, 14th Indian Cooperative Congress *Background Papers,* Sept. 2001, p. 337.
4. *Ibid.,* p. 339.
5. NCUI, *Indian Cooperative Movement—A Statistical Profile-2009,* pp. 98-99.

9

National Cooperative Housing Federation of India (NCHF)

The cooperative housing movement dates back to the year 1909, when, the first society was set up in Mysore followed by Bombay. However, the existence of cooperative housing societies was negligible till 1950. The first five year plan emphasized its importance and the working group on housing was constituted in 1962 to make comprehensive recommendation for its healthy growth. This group recommended setting up of a national level organization of housing cooperatives for promoting, guiding and coordinating activities of housing cooperatives.[1]

The National Cooperative Housing Society came into existence in 1969 with six state-level federations for promoting, coordinating and facilitating the development of housing cooperatives, along with providing guidance to housing cooperatives and their federations. NCFH is also supported by the Ministry of Housing and Urban Poverty Alleviation which enables them to receive regular grant-in-aid.[2]

In addition to vigorous advocacy and representative role for housing cooperatives, NCHF regularly publishes books and bulletins and undertakes research projects to inform and disseminate information to housing cooperatives, the public agencies and the general public. NCHF has opened a training centre in its premises that delivers courses to member cooperators, directors and staff of federations and housing cooperatives. It also actively organizes educational conferences and provides guidance on technical matters while assisting them in general coordination and supervision of activities.[3]

General Growth of Cooperative Housing Movement in India

Year	*No. of Societies*	*No. of Members (in Million)*	*Working Capital (Rs. In Million)*
1959-60	5,564	0.32	550
1965-66	11,778	0.76	1,410
1971-72	20,234	1.37	5,862
1976-77	29,516	1.80	10,030
1981-82	35,000	2.20	12,000
1983-84	40,000	3.00	15,000
1991-92	70,000	4.50	20,000
1998-99	90,000	6.50	50,000
2002-03	92,000	6.60	55,000

Source: 15th Indian Cooperative Congress, 2008, p.143.

The NCHF also drafted a Model Cooperative Housing Societies Law which has been approved by the Ministry of Urban Employment and Poverty Alleviation and the ministry of Law. The above Model Law has been sent to State Governments and union Territory Administrations with a request to enact their Cooperative Housing Societies Act on the basis of the Model Law keeping in view the local conditions and requirements.[4]

Summary of Organisational Structure, Functions and Progress*

Housing Cooperatives

National Cooperative Housing Federation (1)

State Cooperative Housing Finance Societies/Federations (26)

Primary Cooperative House Building/Group Housing Societies (92,000)

Members (6.60 Million)

Main Functions

National Cooperative Housing Federation

- Coordinate and guide members in planning and construction of houses;
- Procure and supply building materials;
- Publications;
- Liaison with government and other agencies on matters related to housing cooperatives;
- Impart training and education to housing cooperatives;

* NCUI, Indian Cooperative Movement—A Statistical Profile-2009, p.100.

State Cooperative Housing Finance Society/ Federation/Corporation

- Arrange funds from government and other financing agencies and advance to member societies as well as individual members;
- Assess, procure, manufacture building materials and supply to societies;
- Guide and assist in technical, financial and legal matters;

Primary Cooperative House Building/Group Housing Societies

- Secure land, develop it;
- Get financial assistance from apex federations and other financing agencies;
- Construct, allot and manage houses;

Future Approach and New Areas

- To ensure appropriate positioning of housing cooperatives in the liberalized economy, following steps will be taken up to ensure smooth functioning of housing cooperatives.

  i) to speed up various sanctions and requirements concerned authorities will be called upon to introduce a single window system at state level;

  ii) to persuade the state governments to adopt the model law on housing cooperatives as approved by the Government of India at the instance of NCHF.

  iii) To facilitate construction of more and more houses for the people of low income group and weaker section;

iv) Efforts will continue to provide more finances to housing cooperatives from the major lending institutions on reduced rate of interest and with procedural simplification;

v) To facilitate setting up of multi purpose cooperatives of urban poor and slum dwellers in various states;

vi) To persuade state governments to allot one-third of the developed land to housing coops on priority at institutional rates.[5]

NOTES

1. Khurana, M.L. "Progress and Problems of Housing Cooperatives", 14th Indian Cooperative Congress, *Background Papers,* NCUI, p. 295.
2. Khurna, M.L. "Housing Cooperatives in India", 15th Indian Cooperative Congress, *Background Papers,* NCUI, p. 57.
3. M. L. Khurna, *Ibid.,* p. 57.
4. M. L. Khurna, "Progress, Problems and Trends of Housing Cooperatives", *15th Indian Cooperative Congress, 2008,* NCUI, p. 149.
5. NCUI, *Indian Cooperative Movement-A Statistical Profile-2009,* p. 100.

10

National Cooperative Dairy Federation of India (NCDFI)

The growth and success of the dairy cooperatives have made them the back bone of the Indian diary industry. The dairy cooperatives have firmly established a viable self generating business that is the country's largest rural employment programme. They have contributed to making India the largest milk producer in the world. The cooperative dairy industry has some third generation fully automated dairies – with bulk chillers being installed in the villages – capable of producing world quality milk products.[1]

The NCDFI came into existence in 1970 with the objectives, to promote the dairy industry and the oilseeds, vegetable/edible oil and vanaspati industry and other commodities on cooperative lines; and to coordinate, help, develop and facilitate the working of the dairy and oilseeds growers' cooperatives and affiliated organizations dealing in commodities.

During the year 2009-10, the National Cooperative Dairy Federation of India Ltd. (NCDFI) continued to coordinate marketing of milk, milk products and frozen semen doses at about 163 defence units which include ASC Depots, Air Force Stations and Military Farms under the Ministry of Defence (MoD) and supply of about 530 MT butter fresh valued at about Rs. 10 crore from the cooperative dairies to about to about 163 defence units. Also it coordinated supply of about 3.41 crore litres of UHT (Tetrapak) Milk to 68 Defence units in Eastern, Western, Northern and Southern Commands valued at about Rs. 124 crores and supply of about 5511 MT of milk products valued at about Rs. 74 crores total the NCDFI coordinated milk and milk products supplies worth of Rs. 339 crores during the year 2009-10.

With a view to make available good quality semen doses to the milk producers in the country, NCDFI has been functioning as 'carrying and forwarding agency' of Frozen semen Doses (FSDs) and embryos.

India has become the world's largest milk producing nation. Despite of achieving this, India is set to face milk shortage due to low productivity and rising consumption in both rural and urban areas. Demand for milk in the country is increasing at much faster rate than its production. High cost of feed and fodder increased the cost of milk production. Many of our milk producers are women and most of whom are landless, small and marginal farmers. For achieving the noble cause of rural upliftment through cooperative dairy development and to check the milk prices in the country, it is important that the Government should have policies that facilitate dairy development. Recently, our dairy cooperatives and the NCDFI had made a strong plea to the Government to consider the necessary policy changes in taxes, export duty and subsidies.[2]

In our country, women play the major role in dairying, it is the women who usually looks after the cattle. Now, in many cases her participation as a dairy cooperative member has given her a degree of economic independence she never had earlier. Over 7,000 village dairy cooperatives are now run by women. Almost two million women belong to dairy cooperatives. However, this membership is currently only a little over 21 percent of the total, and the aim is to increase it is to 50 percent by 2010.[3]

The Operation Flood programme was implemented in three phases. The first phase started on 1st July 1970 and was officially terminated on 31st March, 1918. The second phase was completed in 1986 and the third phase was closed on 30th April, 1996.During the three phases, a total investment of more than Rs. 1700 crore was made. Half of this amount was spent in creating rural processing facilities. About twenty two percent was used for creating urban marketing facilities and another twelve percent was utilized for enhancing milk production. The balance amount was invested in creating facilities for training, research and cooperative education.[4]

Together dairy cooperatives handle about 17 percent of marketable surplus of milk in the country. About 8 percent is controlled by organized private trade. The rest is traded in unorganized market. In the coming years, dairy cooperatives are expected to retain this market share. Dairy cooperatives are even expected to improve their share in milk procurement by developing infrastructure for procurement, processing, transportation and marketing.[5]

Main Functions

National Cooperative Dairy Federation

- Attempts are being made to develop competence in proving information technology services to the members in future;
- Developing superior network of the dairy cooperatives for inter diary online communication for speedy and effective decision making;

Summary of Organisational Structure, Functions and Progress*

Dairy Cooperatives

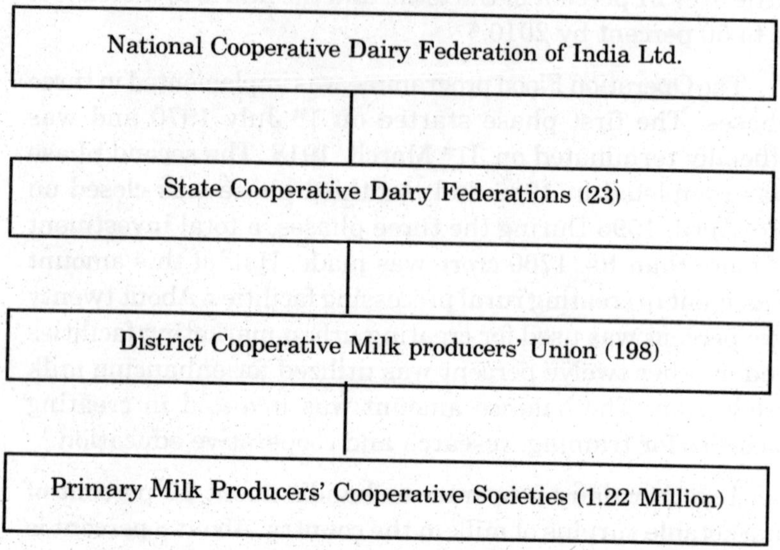

- Improving quality of services to the members in terms of speed and effectiveness;
- Fast dissemination of information to help the members in timely and appropriate decision making;
- Advocacy with the dairy cooperatives for supply of milk and milk products to defence services;
- Coordination with the Indian Railways for allotment of milk parlours to the dairy cooperatives;
- Research, Publication and consultancy on dairying;
- Liaison with NDDB, government of India, etc.

---

* NCUI, Indian cooperative Movement—A Statistical Profile-2009, p. 101.

State Cooperative Dairy Federations

- Production programming;
- Marketing of milk products;
- Coordinating bulk purchases;
- Assist the unions in input programmes;
- Training, consultancy etc.

District Cooperative Milk Producers' Union

- Organization and supervision of primary cooperative societies;
- Collect milk from primaries for processing and manufacturing milk products;
- Ensure regular payment of DCS;
- Marketing liquid milk in their area of operation;
- Distribution of cattle feed;
- Provide technical inputs;
- Arrange training of staff, DCS personnel;
- Educate member farmer and farmer ladies

Primary Milk Producers' Cooperative Society

- Collection and sale of milk to milk unions;
- Ensure regular and remunerative payment to producers;
- Help members to increase milk production;
- Provide veterinary first aid and artificial Insemination services;
- Sale of cattle feed.[6]

NOTES

1. Ravi Shankar, "Progress and Problems of Dairy Cooperatives", 14th Indian Cooperative Congress, *Background Papers,* NCUI, p. 303.
2. NCUI, *Annual Report, 2009-10,* p. 68.
3. Ravi Shankar, "Role and Vision of Dairy Cooperatives in New Millennium", 15th Indian Cooperative Congress, *Background Papers,* p. 46.
4. R. N. Ghatak, "Reforms Initiative – Vision of Dairy Cooperatives for Autonomous and Competitive Functioning", 15th Indian Cooperative Congress, *Background Papers,* p.63.
5. *Ibid.,* p.67.
6. NCUI, *Indian cooperative Movement A Statistical Profile-2009,* p.101.

11

National Federation of Urban Cooperative Bank and Credit Society Ltd. (NFUCBCS)

The institutional rural credit system for agriculture comprises of (1) Short-term and Long-term Cooperative Credit Institutions, (2) Commercial Banks (3) Regional Rural banks, (4) National Bank for Agriculture and Rural Development and (5) Reserve Bank of India. The Institutional Credit delivery System for urban areas comprises of (1) Commercial Banks (2) Urban Cooperative Banks and (3) Urban Cooperative Credit Societies.

The Cooperative Credit Structure consists of two wings namely short term and long term. The short term cooperative credit structure deals with medium term credit also for agricultural purposes and it is federal in character. It is mostly based on a three tier pattern with the SCBs at the Apex Level, DCCBs at the intermediary level and PACS at the village level.[1]

Cooperative Credit Societies are mainly operating in the urban areas. They are spread even in small towns. Their operations are less complicated than those of full fledged banks and they cater to the requirements of limited group of individuals who are their members. A large number of cooperative credit societies are formed by well identified community groups. Most of them do not face any serious problems except that many of the general restrictive provisions of the Cooperative Societies Act of the states also constrict their operations. Striking features of these societies is that most of their members come from middle class.

Another class of cooperative credit societies is that of salary earners societies. A very large number of corporates both in the public as well as the private sector where a sizeable number of employees work, generally have their own credit societies which are managed by the staff themselves. There are very big societies of this nature, particularly in the Railways, P & T, ports and many large public sector undertakings. Some of these salary earner societies have earlier been converted into banks.[2]

To represent the cooperative credit banking institutions of the country the *National Federation of Urban Cooperative Bank and Credit Society Ltd.* came into existence. NAFCUM is the apex level promotional body of urban cooperative banks and credit societies of the country. There are 1721 urban cooperative banks (UCBs) and around 40,000 credit societies meeting the credit needs of about 50 million members that are spread throughout the country and are helping in financial inclusion.[3] The urban cooperative banks and credit societies are facing a member of problems e.g., Competition with other banks, improving the image of cooperative banks, management of investment portfolio, challenges of retail banking, challenges of deregulation and information technology.

The NAFCB has drawn a long term performance programme to overcome such problems. Research studies on relevant issues have been given priority inclusing financing of Ph.D. work of Universities in the field of its interest. Also training programmes have been strengthened and matters concerning taxes have been brought into the notice of Finance Minister.

Summary of Organisational Structure Functions and Progress*

National Federation of Urban Cooperative Banks and Credit Societies Ltd.

Non-Agricultural Credit Cooperatives
Urban Credit Cooperatives

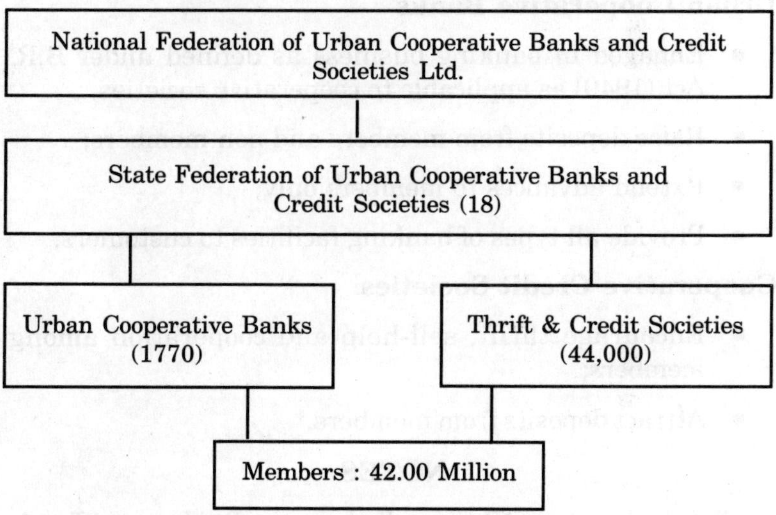

Main Functions

National Federation of Urban Cooperatives Banks and Credit Societies

- Promotion and strengthing of urban cooperative credit sector;

*NCUI, Indian Cooperative Movement – A Statistical Profile 2009, p. 102.

- Human Resource Development (HRD) of member organizations through training programmes/seminars/ workshops/study tours.
- Banking and cooperative information services;
- Research in credit sector;
- Propogation of cooperative credit, image building through publication and publicity;
- International cooperative relations with ICA/ICBA/IRU/ WOCCU
- Cooperative Planning;

Urban Cooperative Banks

- Engaged in banking business as defined under B.R. Act (1949) as applicable to cooperative societies;
- Raise deposits from members and non-members;
- Extend advances to members only;
- Provide all types of banking facilities to customers;

Cooperative Credit Societies:

- Encourage thrift, self-help and cooperation among members;
- Attract deposits from members.[4]

NOTES

1. B. Subrahmanyam, "Progress, Performance, Problems and Trends in Cooperative Credit and Banking Institutions", 14th Indian Cooperative Congress, *Background Papers,* NCUI, p. 251.
2. B. Krishna, "Progress and Problems of Urban Cooperative Banking and Credit Sector", 14th Indian Cooperative Congress, *Background Papers,* NCUI, pp. 271-272.
3. "Brief Reports of National Level Cooperative Organizations", *NCUI, Annual Report,* 2009-10, pp. 66-67.
4. NCUI, *Indian Cooperative Movement – A Statistical Profile 2009,* p.102.

12

National Labour Cooperatives Federation of India Ltd.

After independence later Prime Minister Pandit Nehru encouraged the cooperatives as an agency for rural development. Even, at the beginning of Five-year Plan in our country, it was also decided that executing agencies at grass root level would be the institutions like Bharat Sewak Samaj, Panchayat and Labour Cooperatives. The National Advisory Board on Labour Cooperatives was constituted in the year 1974 and subsequently named as National Advisory Council on Labour Cooperatives under the Chairmanship of Hon'ble Minister for Agriculture during 1986. This National body has been reviewing the progress of Labour Cooperatives and the Government policies.

The Government of India has been taking keen interest in improving the socio-economic conditions of labour cooperatives. A National Advisory Council on Labour Cooperatives has reconstituted again under the Chairmanship of Union Minister of Agriculture on 10-06-2003.[1]

The Government of India observed that there had been a large scale exploitation of forest labour, tribals and other construction workers by the private contractors. The workers by and large belongs to weaker sections of the society. Labour Cooperatives were, therefore, accepted as one of the media to check this exploitation. Since then the Central as well as the State Governments have been adopting supporting policies for promotion of labour cooperatives for the socio economic development of their members. In order to coordinate the activities of labour cooperatives in different States and to influence the national policies for their development, need for an apex organization gave birth to *National Labour Cooperatives Federation of India Ltd. (NLCF).*[2]

National Labour Cooperatives Federations of India (NLCF) was organized in the year 1981 as an apex organization of labour cooperatives working under the provisions of Multi-State Cooperative Societies Act, 2002. NLCF's main objective is to organize, promote, coordinate, help and develop the working labour cooperatives for economic and social development of the unorganized sector, the poor labourers consisting of economically weaker section of the society mainly SC/St and OBCs.[3]

National Federation of Labour Cooperative Ltd., is working as Chief Spokesman of Labour Cooperative Movement in the country. Main source of finances of this federation is Grant-in-aid received from Government of India, Ministry of Agriculture and annual subscription from its member organizations. However, NFLC is doing its best to promote the Labour Cooperative Movement in the country.[4]

About 42,041 labour Contract/Construction and Forest Labour Cooperatives are in existence in the country with their 215 District and 16 State level Federations having a membership of 26 lakhs member workers. Presently NLCF has membership of 215 Societies/Federations which includes Primary, District and State Federations as on 31.03.2011.[5]

The following figure gives progress of labour cooperative movement in the country.

Progress of Labour Coop. Movement in India

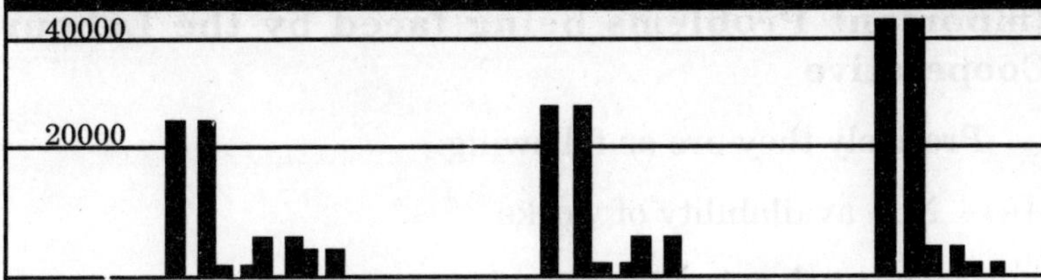

S.No.	Description	1980-81	2001-02	2010-11
1	Number of Societies	14389	32960	42041
2.	Membership (in lakhs)	8.64	20.25	26
3.	Working Capital (in lakhs)	119.17	805.32	-
4.	Buisness Turnover (in Crore)	119.32	1000.35	2250

NLCF is the chief spokesman of Indian Labour Cooperative Movement. It has played a significant role in promoting, organizing the activities of the labour contract/ construction, forest labour cooperatives at certain levels. But the NLCF has been able to make very limited dent in improving the working, living and social conditions of its members and non-members societies.[6]

However, despite its own limitations, because of its dealing with the poorest and weakest the NLCF and NACLS has not been left behind in making its valuable contribution to the cause of the upliftment of weaker sections of the society including that of women cooperatives in its own humble way.

It is supposed to take care of skilled and unskilled labour of which there is mushroom growth in India. Almost 30% of the population living below poverty line cannot be expected to be literate or skilled in any of the activities which may ensure them two square meals, the most modest living etc. not to talk of any standard or average level of living. To ameliorate the lot of this sea of humanity concerted efforts fully supported by the Government in states and centre needs to be focused on the gigantic problems of their employment and livelihood.[7]

Important Problems being faced by the Labour Cooperative

Precisely they are as following:

(a) Non availability of works

The work awarding agencies are reluctant to encourage allotment of works to labour cooperatives, for obvious reasons, inspite of supportive policy of the Government of India.

(b) Supportive policies have been notified by a few states only.

(c) Financial constraints – District Cooperatives Banks are the only agency to provide working capital loan to these cooperatives on formal lending rates, which is ultimately uneconomical for them. There is no provision for long term/short term loans.

(d) Construction industry have become very competitive and use of modern equipment by private contractors is preventing the labour cooperatives to compete with private sectors as they have to borrow them on high rents.[8]

Main Functions

National Labour Cooperatives Federation of India Ltd.

- To organize promote and develop the lab our contract and forest labour cooperatives, their district and /or state level federations;
- To arrange publication of literature, books and periodicals to maintain information bureau, library of labour cooperatives, education, training programme and

Summary of Organisational Structure, Functions and Progress*

Labour Cooperatives

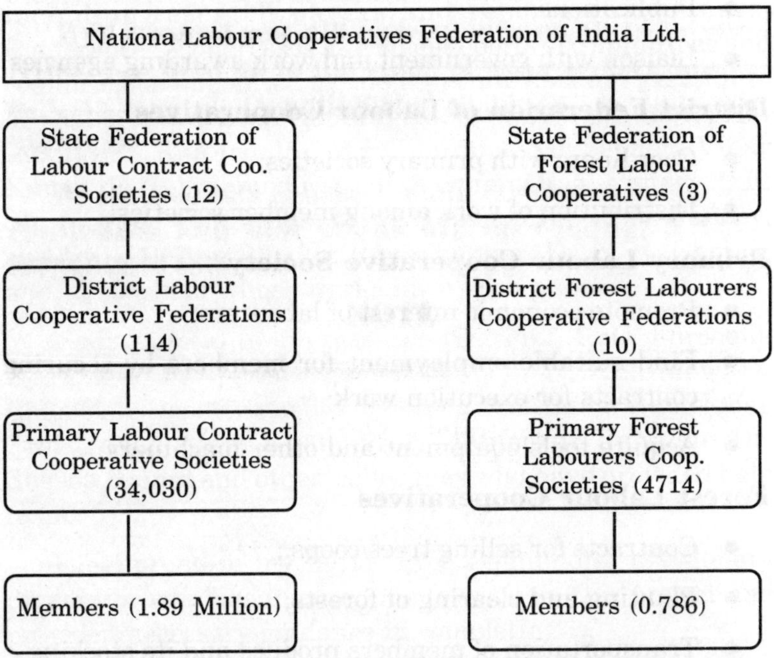

to convene seminars, conferences, exhibitions and to organize, assist, guide and help such activities at state and other level.

- To supply tools, implements, accessories and sophisticated machinery to its members or their affiliated societies on hire purchase or hire system.
- To provide Technical know-how and technology to members;
- To represent the cause of labour cooperative movement at various levels;

---

* NCUI, Indian Cooperative Movement—A Statistical Profile-2009, p. 103.

State Federation of Labour Cooperatives

- Technical guidance to labour cooperatives;
- Provide credit facilities to primary societies;
- Publications;
- Liaison with government and work awarding agencies.

District Federation of Labour Cooperatives

- Coordinate with primary societies;
- Distribution of work among member societies;

Primary Labour Cooperative Society

- Promote economic interest of labourers;
- Find suitable employment for members by securing contracts for execution work;
- Acquire tools equipment and other machinery;

Forest Labour Cooperatives

- Contracts for selling trees/coops.;
- Planting and clearing of forests;
- Transportation of members produce and its stocking.

Future Approach

- To promote state, district level cooperative labour federations in the state where such structure do not exist;
- To organize primary labour contract and forest labour cooperatives in the country particularly in North Eastern Region;
- To set its own vocational training centre to work as nodal agency for providing the training to unskilled labourers with the financial assistance of Ministry of Agriculture, Government of India;

- To promote the economic interests of its members including their affiliated societies vis-à-vis National Federation to obtain work from work awarding agencies and executing through labour cooperatives, to improve the financial position of National Federation and to provide the regular work to member labour cooperatives round the year;

New Areas

- Organization of new state, district and primary labour and forest labour cooperative societies;
- Creation of resource centre in the NLCF's office to provide latest statistical datas;
- To cover village artisans like barbers, washer-man, cobblers, blacksmiths, hawkers under the fold of labour cooperatives.[9]

NOTES

1. R. N. Pandey, "Labour Cooperatives for Employment Generation in present scenario of globalization and Liberalization", *15th Indian Cooperative Congress,* 2008, NCUI, pp. 69-70.
2. www.labcofed.org.
3. R. N. Pandey, "Problems and Prospects of Labour Cooperatives", *15th Indian Cooperative Congress 2008*, NCUI, p. 157.
4. P. K. Shrawat, "Progress and Problems of Labour Cooperatives and its Role for Development of Weaker Sections", 14th Indian Cooperative Congress, *Background papers,* NCUI, p. 302.
5. www.labcofed.org.
6. R. N. Pandey, *Op.cit.,* p. 71.
7. *Ibid.,* p. 71.
8. P. K. Shrawat, *Op.cit.,* p. 300.
9. NCUI, *Indian Cooperative Movement A Statistical Profile-2009,* p. 103.

13

National Federation of Fisherment Cooperative Ltd. (FISHCOPFED)

In order to develop and ensure sustainable livelihood and welfare of fishermen in particular the *National Fisheries Development Board (NFDB) was established in 2006.*

FISHCOPFED needs to train at least 10,000 fishers per year with an aim to build capacity of fishers, enhance the production and thereby provide economic empowerment and livelihood support to the poor fishers which is the ultimate objective and mandate of FISHCOPFED.

This calls of enhanced involvement of FISHCOPFED in the programmes of the ministry as well as NFDB, not only for training component alone but also direct implementation of certain other programmes leading to empowerment of fishermen and fisherwomen in the country.[1]

There is a need for revitalization of fisheries cooperatives for which FISHCOPFED must take the lead, its activities being an interface between the governmental programmes and fisheries cooperative activities on the ground. An action plan has to be devised by the federation with an aim to explore ways and means of strengthening and capacity building of the fisheries cooperatives on a priority basis.[2]

FISHCOPFED has to strongly focus on professionalized management of its activities and undertake a lead role in providing directions to the fisheries cooperatives in the country on a continuous basis.

The federation is an ideal forum to create, disseminate and manage an integrated database and information networking on fisheries cooperatives sector to benefit all stakeholders at large. It can productively provide market intelligence activities, which will benefit the poor fishermen in many ways. FISHCOPFED in turn needs to build and upgrade its own capacity to qualitatively deliver these services more effectively.[3]

With the Primary Membership of more than 19.38 lakhs fishermen the present structure of fishermen cooperatives in India is as under: [4]

National Level Federation	1
State Level Federation	
Central (District/Regional)	17
Level Federations	18
Primary Societies	12,427

- Transfer of intermediate technology of fishers through cooperatives;
- Providing insurance cover to over 29 lakh fisher members through Centrally Sponsored Group Accident Insurance Scheme-Rs. 1,00,000/- against accidental death or permanent (full) disability and/or Rs. 50,000 against permanent (partial) disability to the nominee/ insured.

- Supply of fish to Delhi based ITDC Hotels and quality fish to consumers in Delhi;
- Arranging inter-state marketing of fish and establishing post-harvest Infrastructure;
- Supply of inputs and fishery requisites;
- Publishing of in-house bi-lingual quarterly for free distribution among members and concerned departments;
- Conduct on in-dept studies on different aspects of fisheries;
- Collect, compile and disseminate data on fishery cooperatives;
- Providing consultancy to fishery cooperatives for formation of projects/schemes;
- Promotion of fishery exports;
- Providing Education and Training to fisher members under NFDB funding;
- Setting up of demonstration-cum-production fishery units.[5]

FISHCOPFED is implementing the Centrally-sponsored Group accident Insurance Scheme for active fishermen in the country covering over 29 lakh fishers. It covers all active fishers by caste of profession in the age group of 18-70 years. At present a cover of Rs. One lakh is provided for accidental death or permanent disability and Rs. 50,000/- for permanent (partial) disability against a premium of Rs. 14/- by the state and Rs. 14/- by the centre.[6]

Women play a very important role in fisheries cooperatives. Once the fishermen bring in the catch, their job begins. Cooperative law does not allow membership of both husband and wife, which prevents women from participating in the management of the fisheries, cooperatives. Women involved in the fishery activities must participate in the management of fisheries cooperatives. The Ardhanarees-waran Committee has recommended joint membership of husband and wife in cooperatives. This may be implemented.[7]

Summary of Organisational Structure, Functions and Progress*

Fisheries Cooperatives

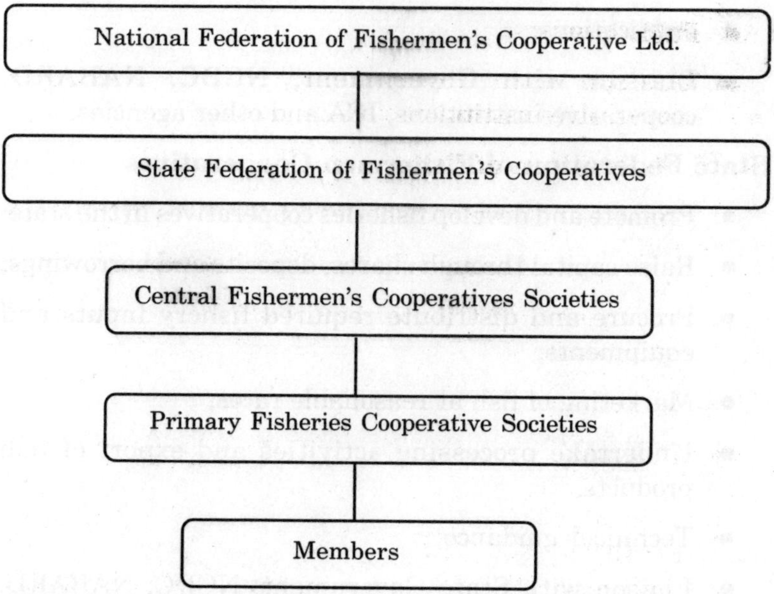

Main Functions

National Federation of Fishermen's Cooperatives

- Arrange supply of fisheries inputs and equipments;
- Transfer technology to fishermen through cooperatives;

* NCUI, Indian Cooperative Movement – A Statistical Profile 2009, p. 104.

- Insurance cover to fishermen
- Procure pond/lake on lese basis for development of fish breed and sale of fish at reasonable price;
- Provide consultancy services to the members of fishery cooperatives;
- Setting-up training-cum-demonstration units;
- Marketing of fish and fish seed and promote exports;
- Research and consultancy in fishery cooperative;
- Publications;
- Liaison with Government, NCDC, NABARD, cooperative institutions, ICA and other agencies;

State Federation of Fishermen Cooperatives

- Promote and develop fisheries cooperatives in the state;
- Raise capital through shares, deposits and borrowings;
- Procure and distribute required fishery inputs and equipments;
- Marketing of fish at reasonable rates;
- Undertake processing activities and export of fish products;
- Technical guidance;
- Liaison with State Government, NCDC, NABARD, FISHCOPFED, FFDA, cooperative banks and other concerned agencies;

Primary Fisheries Cooperatives

- Motivate fishermen to organize cooperatives;
- Procure fish from members and provide complete infrastructure for sale of fish;
- Provide fish seed, net and other inputs and equipments;

- Arrange technical guidance for members;

Future Approach

- Project Management;
- Trade development through partnership;
- Online Services to members;

New Areas

- Human Resource Development and Management;
- Restructuring and revitalizing potential members;
- Project consultancy.[8]

NOTES

1. K. V. Thomas, "Development of Cooperative Fish Marketing and Achievements – Some Issues", *Cooperator, December, 2009,* p. 263-64.
2. *Ibid.,* p. 264.
3. *Ibid.,* p. 264.
4. M. M. Tewary, "Revitalisation of Non-Viable/Weak Cooperatives with Special Reference to Fishermen Cooperatives", 14th Indian Cooperative Congress, *Background Papers,* NCUI, p. 99.
5. *FISHCOOPS, Vol. 22,* No. January-March, 2010, p. 14.
6. *FISHCOOPS, Vol. 22,* No. January-March, 2010, p. 29.
7. M. M. Tewary, *Op.cit.,* p. 107.
8. NCUI, *Indian Cooperative Movement – A Statistical Profile 2009,* p. 104.

14

National Federation of Cooperative Sugar Factories Ltd. (NFCSF)

In pursuant of national policy adopted by the Government, the cooperative movement branched out into all spheres of activity and has made significant progress in various segments of Indian economy.

Amongst the cooperative sector, sugar cooperatives is one of the most successful sector and the success of it mainly due to the adherence of the federal structure.[1]

The birth and evolution of cooperative sugar factories took place in the second quarter of the last century. Since then they have it has made remarkable progress. Today there are about 251 working cooperative sugar factories in the country producing around 60 percent of the total national production. These cooperative sugar factories have also contributed to the socio-economic development of the surrounding rural community by providing irrigation facilities, agricultural extension and education, health and recreation facilities. Sugar cooperatives have thus acted as a catalyst for industrilisation and overall development for the rural masses.[2]

Sugarcane is the backbone of the sugar industry and the success of any sugar factory will depend on the availability of good variety of sugarcane-rich in sugar content-and adequate quantity of sugarcane to utilize the capacity of the individual factories to the full extent. To improve the quality and per hectare yield of sugarcane, technologies developed by various research organizations in the country and abroad will have to be transferred to the farmers fields, particularly the low cost technology and new varieties, to suit millions of small sugar cane growers.[3]

The industry, of which the total turnover is around Rs. 30,000 crores, contributes about Rs. 18,000 crores annually to be the national exchequer and treasuries of various states governments by way of excise duty and purchase tax on sugarcane. Out of this, the cooperative sector of the sugar industry accounts for about Rs. 1,000 crores.[4] During 1982, 1988 to 1993, 1996 and 2000 India was the largest producer of sugar.

Many sugar factories have set up industries based on the main by-products i.e., bagasse and molasses. Plants have been set up for production of different kinds of paper, newsprint, particle board, fulrfural from bagasse and distilleries have been set up for production of ethanol, ethyl alcohol, carbon dioxide, alcohol based chemical plants, plans for production of yeast, lactic acid, ephydrine etc. from molasses.

One of the drawbacks of the cooperative sector of the sugar industry has been the bureaucratic control of the sugar cooperatives in majority of the States. This has hindered the progress and development of sugar cooperatives. Many of the sugar cooperatives are still governed by the Government Administrations.[5]

The *National Federation of Cooperatives Sugar Factories* was established in 1960. The NFCSF has been taking up the routine problems of member factories with the Government and other central authorities for their logical solution, assisting and guiding them in all sugar policy, technical, financial, managerial and legal matters. Over and above customary services, the experts of NFCSF in the disciplines of sugar engineering, sugar technology, sugarcane agronomy, financial management and manpower planning guided and helped the member sugar factories to adopt new technologies and methods for cost effective production of sugarcane and effective utilization of by-products of the industry for its value addition.

During the year 2009-10, the federation undertook eight rehabilitation, modernization and expansion projects, five co-generation projects, one project of bio-methanation of spent wash, a report for valuation and modernization and balancing for raw sugar defecto remelt process, revised project report for two sugar plants and detailed project report for one new sugar factory and provided technical consultancy and inspection services for five factories.[6]

Summary of Organisational Structure, Functions and Progress*

Sugar Cooperatives

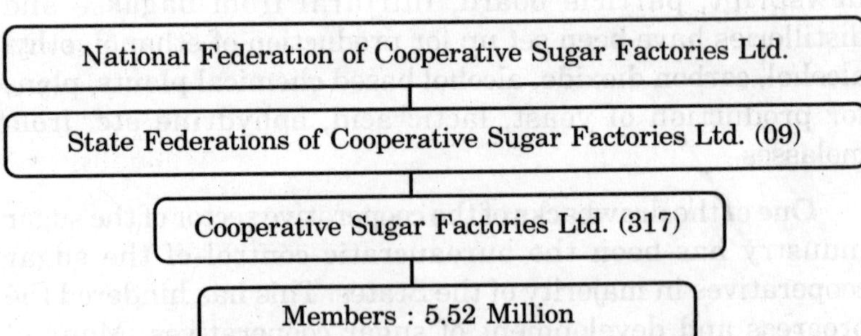

* NCUI, Indian Cooperative Movement – A Statistical Profile 2009, p. 105.

Main Functions

National Federation of Cooperative Sugar Factories Ltd.

- Promotes and develops cooperatives of sugarcane growers and provides support, services and guidance to its affiliated cooperative sugar factories and state federations of cooperative sugar factories for their efficient and sustained working by;
- Promoting and safequarding the interests of its members in accordance with the cooperative principles;
- Arranging education and training for the benefit of its members;
- Arranging technical support and services to its members both for improving their operational efficiency as well as for organization and promotion of new cooperative sugar factories;
- Promoting R & D activities for its members, sponsoring research projects, conferences, seminars etc. to find out solutions of the problems of its member cooperative sugar factories and allied subjects;
- Acts as accredited representative and spokesman organization of the sector of cooperative sugar factories at the policy for a of Central and State Governments, business for a and organizations relating to sugar industry; establishing liaison with national and international organizations and others allied to sugar industry;
- Advising and assisting members on matters relating to their management and operations;
- Undertaking information services for the benefit of members;

- Publishing literature and documents on sugar industry for the benefit of members;
- Undertaking all other activities that are incidental and conducive to the attainment of objectives and interest of members for the development and progress of sugar and its co-products industries either directly or through strategically collaborative joint ventures or partnerships with other organizations including insurance;

State Federations of Cooperative Sugar Factories

- Advices and help in promotion of cooperative sugar factories in their respective states and coordinate and facilitate their working;
- Plays a very important role as mediator with the state governments for their members' activities;
- Assists in securing necessary financial accommodation from respective state governments and cooperative banks;
- Helps in the sale of the produce of its members

Cooperative Sugar Factories

- Procure sugar cane from members and pay remunerative prices
- Improve sugar cane cultivation and provide inputs, produce sugar and by-products;
- Mobilise deposits from members;
- Other development activities for members.[7]

NOTES

1. Vinay Kumar, "Progress and Problems of Sugar Cooperatives in India", 14th Indian Cooperative Congress, *Background Papers,* NCUI, p. 291.

2. Vinay Kumar, "Role and Vision of Sugar Cooperatives in the New Millennium", 14th Indian Cooperative Congress, *Background Papers,* NCUI, p. 33.
3. *Ibid.,* p. 33.
4. Vinay Kumar, "Progress, Problems and Trends in the Development of Sugar Cooperatives", *15th Indian Cooperative Congress, 2007-08,* p. 133.
5. *Ibid.,* pp. 134-135.
6. "Brief Reports of National Level Cooperative Organizations", NCUI *Annual Report,* 2009-10, p. 66.
7. NCUI, *Indian Cooperative Movement – A Statistical Profile 2009,* p. 105.

15

National Heavy Engineering Cooperative Ltd.

Established nearly 25 years ago as a national co-operative, NHEC, a one-of-its-kind organization at the national level, is promoted by the national co-operative development corporation (NCDC), Govt. of India, and supported by the national federation of co-operative sugar factories (apex body of the Indian co-operative sugar factories). All these came together to help India gain self sufficiency in the supply and modernization of sugar plants.

To bring the promoter's dreams in reality and to achieve the estimated goals, NHEC acquired a good piece of land to start its operations at Talegaon Dabhade, 35 kms. From Pune city and approximately 160 kms. From Mumbai in Maharashtra 1980 saw NHEC start its production operations at the works.

In the fast paced markets of the 90s, NHEC advanced into much more than a sugar machinery manufacturer. NHEC proved itself with excellent infrastructure that worked at providing universal solutions in many other fields.

At NHEC future plans encompass the manufacture of Sugar Refinery, Bulk Handling Material, High Pressure

Boilers, Steam Turbines, Chemical/Petrochemical, Ore Benefactors, Oil Exploration and Mining Equipment.

NHEC is also gearing up to work for Nuclear, Atomic, Coal Handling and other vital national/international projects.

Well groomed and still growing in strength and stature, NHEC has lived up to the vision of its promoters, and the expectations of its millions of customers in India and worldwide.

As the frontiers of today's world are changing fast, new challenges and new vistas are up coming, NHEC's commitment endures.[1]

NOTE

1. www.indiamart.com/nh-engineering.

16

The All India Federation of Cooperative Spinning Mills Ltd. (AIFCOSPIN)

The *All Indian Federation of Cooperative Spinning Mill Ltd. (AIFCOSPIN) was established* **in 1964** with the specific objective of providing all assistance and guidance for establishing new spinning cooperatives and for expansion and modernization of the existing ones. Around this period, the National Cooperative Development Corporation (NCDC) also framed policies for encouraging the growth of the cooperative spinning sector by providing financial assistance and advisory services. These favourable developments impacted a new vigour to the cooperative spinning sector, which registered steady and impressive growth during 1970's and 1980's. Currently, there are about 158 cooperative spinning mills dispersed in 16 States and Union Terrorists. Their installed capacity is around 3.46 million spindles and 18,310 open end rotors, constituting nearly 11 percent of the country's total.[1]

The establishment of the All Indian Federation of Cooperative Spinning Mills Ltd., (AIFCOSPIN) was necessary to provide much needed technical expertise and guidance for establishing new mills and run the existing ones efficiently.[2] AIFCOSPIN is playing a key role in the growth of the cooperative spinning sector in the country. However, AIFCOSPIN has been finding it more and more difficult to provide such services without adequate compensation from members. A strong AIFCOSPIN is essential for the sector itself to be strong and in turn a robust sector is crucial for the strength of AIFCOSPIN.[3]

Vision of the cooperative spinning sector remains basically the same as was conceived by its founding fathers fifty years ago i.e., to generate maximum additional employment opportunities in rural India by effectively utilizing the raw material produced locally, take as many hand as possible away from the total dependence on agriculture and provide gainful employment in industrial and allied fields, all aimed at augmenting the income and elevating the quality of life of the economically backward sections of the rural population. However, the dimensions and perspective have now changed with the change in times.[4]

The Federation maintains close liaison with the concerned Government authorities as well as NCDC, NCUI and financial institutes. It conducts seminars, conference to discuss changing needs of the industry and improve its competence. During the last year a delegation of the federation also visited the Union Ministers of agriculture to discuss problems and find out their solution. During 20008-09 it had launched a new specialize service known as Machine Maintenance Audit (MMA) and last year undertook special studies of a mill and made suggestions for improvement.

Summary of Organisational Structure, Functions and Progress*

Spinning Cooperatives

All India Federation of Cooperative Spinning Mills

State Federations of Cooperative Spinning Mills

Cooperative Spinning Mills

Members : 0.771 Million
(Weavers + Growers)

Main Functions

All India Federation of Cooperative Spinning Mills

- Plan, formulate and implement projects for establishment, expansion and modernization of spinning mills;
- Technical consultancy in textiles and yarn market surveys;
- Turn-key consultancy for World Bank-NCKC integrated ginning and spinning projects;

* NCUI, Indian Cooperative Movement—A Statistical Profile 2009, p. 106.

- Training in cotton and yarn testing;
- Liaison with central and state governments, NCDC, banks and central financing institutions;
- Publications

State Cooperative Spinning Mills Federation

- Coordinate and facilitate the working of members mills;
- Assist in promotion and organization of new mills in cooperative sector;
- Provide technical know-how;
- Arrange supply of raw materials, storage facilities;

Cooperative Spinning Mills

- Produce yarn and supply to weaver apex cooperative federations.[5]

NOTES

1. S. J. Sequeria, "Revitalising the Cooperative Spinning Sector", 14th Indian Cooperative Congress, *Background Papers,* NCUI, p. 107.
2. S. J. Sequeira, "Cooperative Spinning Sector-Progress and Prospects", *15th Indian Cooperative Congress, 2008,* NCUI, p. 137.
3. S. J. Sequeria, *Op.cit.,* pp. 110-111.
4. S. J. Sequeira, "Reforms Initiative – Vision of Spinning Cooperative for Autonomous and Competitive Functioning", *15th Indian Cooperative Congress,* 2008, NCUI, p. 56.
5. NCUI, *Indian Cooperative Movement-A Statistical Profile 2009,* p. 106.

17

All India Hundloom Fabrics Marketing Cooperative Society

Handloom weavers' cooperatives exist since long. The handloom products granted political importance as the products were used by politicians of all status.

The Handloom Cooperative Fabrics marketing Cooperative society promotes handloom products and arranges for its sale. The federation has a pyramidal structure and functions for the development of marketing of products. The below given chart explains its organizational structure and other activities.

Main Functions

All India Handloom Cooperative Fabrics Marketing Cooperative Society

- Promote domestic and export market for products by handloom cooperatives;
- Arrange marketing of finished goods;
- Arrange exhibitions;

Summary of Organisational Structure, Functions and Progress*

Weavers' Cooperatives

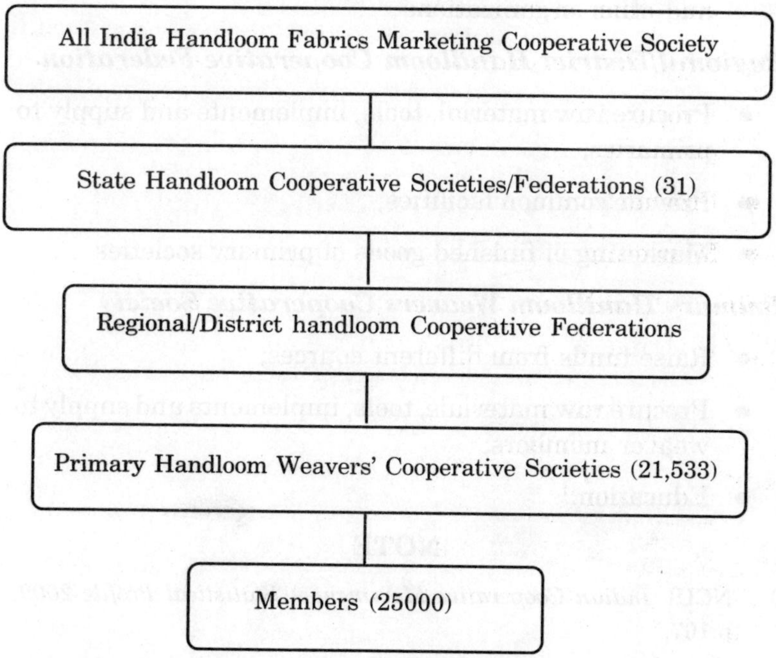

- Publications;
- Liaison with government, NCDC, NABARD KVIC, All India Handloom Board, cooperative institutions and other organizations.

State Handloom Cooperative Society/Federation

- Procure raw materials, tools and supply to member institutions;
- Marketing of finished goods of members by obtaining orders;
- Organise exhibitions;

- Publications;
- Technical Training/Education;
- Liaison with Govt., NABARD, NCDC, Cooperative bank and other organizations

Regional/District Handloom Cooperative Federation

- Procure raw material, tools, implements and supply to primaries;
- Provide common facilities;
- Marketing of finished goods of primary societies

Primary Handloom Weavers Cooperative Society

- Raise funds from different sources;
- Procure raw materials, tools, implements and supply to weaver members;
- Education.[1]

NOTE

1. NCUI, *Indian Cooperative Movement-A Statistical Profile 2009*, p.107.

18

National Cooperative Tobacco Growers' Federation Limited

The National Cooperatives Tobacco Growers' Federation came into existence to promote non-verginie tobacco growers cooperatives and explore market for them as given in the chart.

Summary of Organisational Structure, Functions and Progress

Tobacco Growers' Cooperatives

National Cooperative Tobacco Growers' Federation (1)

State Cooperative Tobacco Growers' Federations (3)

Primary Tobacco Growers' Cooperatives (217)

Members (25000)

Main Functions

- Promote non-virginia tobacco growers' cooperatives;
- Explore market for tobacco;
- Local and overseas.[1]

NOTE

1. NCUI, Indian Cooperative Movement-A Statistical Profile 2009, p. 108.

19

National Tree Grows Cooperative Federation (NTGCF)

The federation came into existence to promote and strengthen village level tree growers cooperative Institutions and assist other village land institutions.

Summary of Organisational Structure, Functions and Progress

Tree Growers' Cooperatives

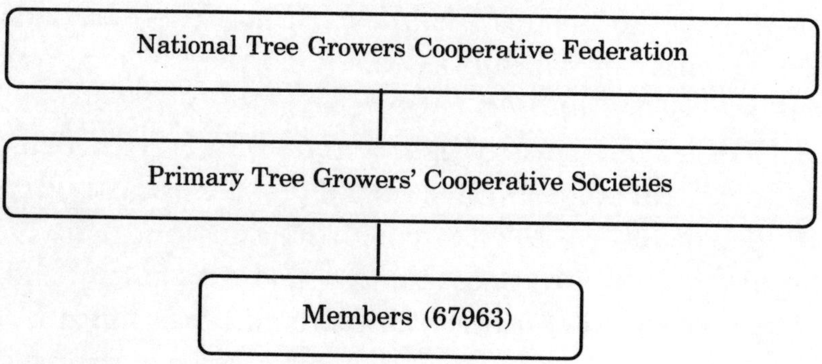

Main Functions

- Promotion and strengthening of village level tree growers' cooperative institutions for governance of common property forests that are diverse, ecologically sound, and which cater to the range of survival needs.[1]

NOTE

1. NCUI, Indian Cooperative Movement-A Statistical Profile 2009, p. 108

International Cooperative Allance*

The International Cooperative Alliance was Founded in London, August 1895. It is an independent, non-governmental organisation which unites, represents and serves co-operatives worldwide. Its registered headquarters, since 1982, is Geneva, Switzerland.

ICA members are national and international co-operative organisations in all sectors of activity including agriculture, banking, fisheries, health, housing, industry, insurance, tourism and consumer co-operatives. Currently, ICA has *269 member organisations* from 97 countries, representing approximately 1 billion individuals worldwide. The following diagram shows total membership of ICA during 1994-2010.

Total Membership 1994-2010

* www.ica.coop/aca/index.html

The region wise percentage of members can be read from the following.

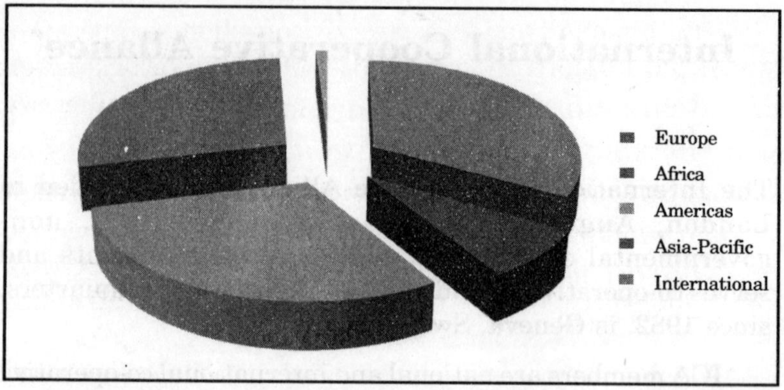

The ICA advocates the interests and success of cooperatives, disseminates best practices and know-how, strengthens their capacity building and monitors their performance and progress over time. It is the custodian of cooperative values and principles and makes the case for their distinctive values based economic business model which also provides individuals and communities with an instrument of self-help and influence over their development.[1]

1. It raises awareness about co-operatives. It helps individuals, government authorities and regional and international institutions understand the co-operative model of enterprise. *ICA is the voice of the co-operative movement.*

2. It ensures that the **right policy environment** exists to enable co-operatives to grow and prosper. It helps its members in their lobbying for new legislation and more appropriate administrative procedures that respect the co-operative model, its principles and values. It provides political support as well as technical expertise to enable co-operatives to compete on a level playing field.

3. It provides its members with key information, best practice and contacts. Through its **publications** it ensures the sharing of information. It organises meetings and workshops to address key issues affecting co-operatives and allows discussion among co-operators from around the world. ICA facilitates contacts between co-operatives for trading purposes and intelligence sharing in a wide range of areas.

4. It provides technical assistance to co-operatives through its **development programme**. ICA promotes capacity-building and financial support, it facilitates job creation and supports poverty reduction and microfinance programmes around the world.[2]

Objects

ICA, a global networking organisation organised at the global, regional, sectoral and thematic levels, is a world-wide representative of co-operative organisations of all kinds that has the following objects:

1. promote the world co-operative movement, based upon mutual self-help and democracy;
2. promote and protect co-operative values and principles;
3. facilitate the development of economic and other mutually beneficial relations between its member organisations;
4. promote sustainable human development and to further the economic and social progress of people, thereby contributing to international peace and security;
5. promote equality between men and women in all decision-making and activities within the co-operative movement.

ICA seeks to obtain its objects in order to achieve its objects at the global, regional, sectoral and thematic levels, the ICA:

a. serves as a forum for exchange of experience and as a source of information on cooperative development, research, and statistics;

b. coordinate actions for the promotion of co-operative development;

c. collaborate with global and regional institutions including the United Nations organisations, and with any other governmental and non-governmental international and national organisations which pursue aims of importance to co-operatives;

d. any other appropriate means.

The ICA is organised at the global, regional, sectoral and thematic levels and comprises the following:

a. a central office;

b. four regions;

   i. ICA Africa

   ii. ICA Americas

   iii. ICA Asia-Pacific

   iv. ICA Europe (incorporated and known as Co-operatives Europe asbl).[3]

The geographic area of each region is as follows:

   i. Africa - open to all member organisations with a head office in Africa and adjacent islands.

   ii. America - open to all member organisations with head office in North, Central and South America, and the Caribbean.

iii. Asia and the Pacific - open to all member organisations with a head office in Asia and the Pacific.

iv. Europe - open to all member organisations with a head office in Europe.

c. global and regional sectoral organisations, and

d. thematic committees.[4]

The organizational structure of ICA is evident from the following chart:

Organizational Structure

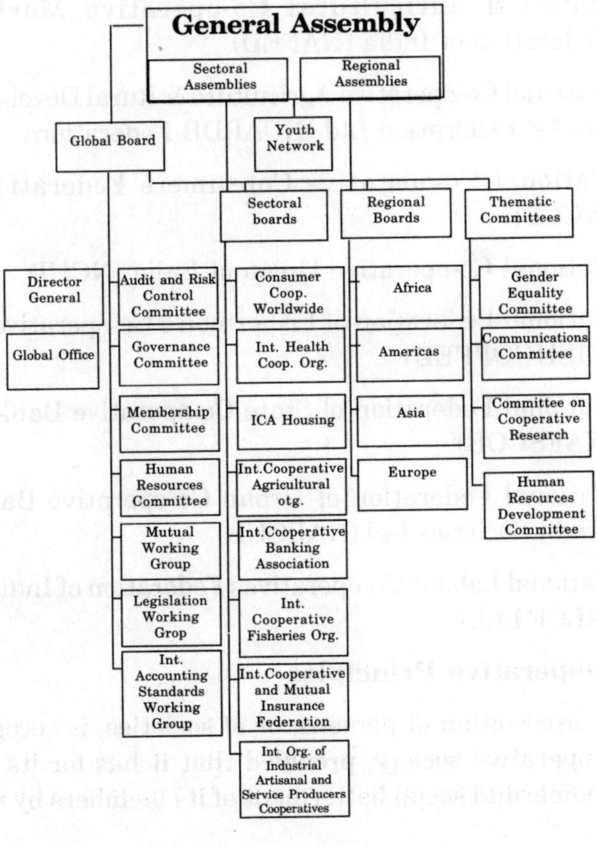

India is one of the members of ICA from Asia Pacific region. The regional office of Asia Pacific is in New Delhi. The following cooperative organizations are member of the ICA from India.

1. Co-operative House Building & Finance Corporation Ltd.
2. Indian Farm Forestry Development Co-operative Ltd. (IFFDC)
3. Indian Farmers Fertiliser Co-operative (IFFCO)
4. Krishak Bharati Co-operative Ltd. (KRIBHCO)
5. National Agricultural Co-operative Marketing Federation of India (NAFED)
6. National Co-operative Agriculture & Rural Development Banks' Federation Ltd (NCARDB Federation)
7. National Co-operative Consumers Federation Ltd (NCCF)
8. National Co-operative Union of India (NCUI)
9. National Federation of Fishermen's Co-operatives Ltd. (FISHCOPFED)
10. National Federation of State Co-operative Banks Ltd. (NAFSCOB)
11. National Federation of Urban Co-operative Banks & Credit Societies Ltd (NAFCUB)
12. National Labour Co-operatives Federation of India, Ltd. (NLCF Ltd.)[5]

ICA Cooperative Principles

Any association of persons, or of societies, is recognised as a co-operative society, provided that it has for its object the economic and social betterment of its members by means of an enterprise based on mutual aid, and that it conforms to the ICA Statement on the Co-operative Identity, as approved by the General Assembly of ICA.

Definition

A co-operative is an autonomous association of persons united voluntarily to meet their common economic, social and cultural needs and aspirations through a jointly-owned and democratically controlled enterprise

Values

Co-operatives are based on the values of self-help, self-responsibility, democracy, equality, equity and solidarity. In the tradition of their founders, co-operative members believe in the ethical values of honesty, openness, social responsibility and caring for others.

Principles

The co-operative principles are guidelines by which co-operatives put their values into practice.

1st Principle: Voluntary and Open Membership

Co-operatives are voluntary organisations, open to all persons able to use their services and willing to accept the responsibilities of membership, without gender, social, racial, political or religious discrimination.[6]

2nd Principle: Democratic Member Control

Co-operatives are democratic organisations controlled by their members, who actively participate in setting their policies and making decisions. Men and women serving as elected representatives are accountable to the membership. In primary co-operatives members have equal voting rights (one member, one vote) and co-operatives at other levels are also organised in a democratic manner.

3rd Principle: Member Economic Participation

Members contribute equitably to, and democratically control, the capital of their cooperative. At least part of that capital is usually the common property of the co-operative. Members usually receive limited compensation, if any, on capital subscribed as a condition of membership. Members allocate surpluses for any or all of the following purposes: developing their co-operative, possibly by setting up reserves, part of which at least would be indivisible; benefiting members in proportion to their transactions with the co-operative; and supporting other activities approved by the membership.

4th Principle: Autonomy and Independence

Co-operatives are autonomous, self-help organisations controlled by their members. If they enter into agreements with other organisations, including governments, or raise capital from external sources, they do so on terms that ensure democratic control by their members and maintain their co-operative autonomy.

5th Principle: Education, Training and Information

Co-operatives provide education and training for their members, elected representatives, managers, and employees so they can contribute effectively to the development of their co-operatives. They inform the general public – particularly young people and opinion leaders – about the nature and benefits of co-operation.

6th Principle: Co-operation among Co-operatives

Co-operatives serve their members most effectively and strengthen the co-operative movement by working together through local, national, regional and international structures.

7th Principle: Concern for Community

Co-operatives work for the sustainable development of their communities through policies approved by their members.[7]

Administration

The ICA Board consists of the President, four Vice-Presidents, and 18 other members, elected by the General Assembly for a four-year term. Vacancies are filled through election at a subsequent General Assembly.

Two of the 18 members of the Board represent the ICA Sectoral Organisations and one represents youth co-operators. These are nominated by their respective constituents based on criteria and terms of reference established by the "ICA Election Committee" and are formally elected by the ICA General Assembly.

The Board meets at least once a year. Meetings may also be called at the request of one-third of the members or by the decision of the President. Decisions may be taken by correspondence.

Members from one country may not have more than one representative on the Board, excluding the President and Vice-Presidents of ICA, Board members representing ICA sectoral organisations and the youth representative, always keeping in mind the representative nature of the Board. This should be monitored by the Election Committee.

No person is entitled to serve on the Board whose organisation is no longer in membership of ICA or is in arrears with its membership subscription fee, or who has ceased to be an accredited representative of the nominating Member or, in the case of Vice-Presidents, of the respective Regional Assembly.

The Board operates in accordance to ICA Board Standing Orders.

Regional Boards

Regional Boards are elected in accordance with the statutes of their region and will consist of at least one

President, and other members elected by the Regional Assembly.

Powers of the Regional Board

Regional boards will

a. work within the global strategic framework of the ICA laid down every four years by the General Assembly;
b. approve within the four-year workplan, budget and redistribution agreements, the annual budget and workplan prepared by the Regional Director for integration into the global budget and workplan for approval by the ICA Board;
c. prepare the agenda and organise the meetings of the Regional Assembly;
d. reinforce member organisations' active participation;
e. in conjunction with the ICA Director-General be responsible for the appointment of the Regional Director;
f. promote sustainable co-operative regional development;
g. build relations between other bodies of the ICA;
h. enhance the image of ICA and the co-operative movement within the region, with national and regional institutions;
i. establish committees and working groups where appropriate;
j. provide recommendations on membership issues from their region to the ICA Board;
k. ensure regional finance and budgeting are strictly monitored and within the general guidelines of ICA.[8]

Regional Directors

Regional Directors are the chief executive officers of the regions, accountable to the elected bodies of the region and responsible for the leadership and efficient management of the regional organisation.

Regional Directors are responsible for:

a. promotion and defence of co-operative values and principles at the regional level;

b. in the framework of the ICA global Strategic Plan, submitting annual work programmes and budgets to be integrated in the overall global workplan and budget of the ICA

c. implementation of the regional Strategic Plan and work programme within the region;

d. representation on request of members organisations' policy concerns to governmental bodies and the public;

e. organisation of the Regional Assemblies and support to elected regional bodies;

f. carrying out any other activities as may be requested by the Director-General or Regional Authorities.

Sectoral Organisations

ICA has eight sectoral organisations which regroup ICA member organisations with specific sectoral interests. Each organisation is democratically governed and financed by the ICA.

- International Co-operative Agricultural Organisation (ICAO)
- International Co-operative Banking Association (ICBA)
- Consumer Co-operatives Worldwide (CCW)

- International Co-operative Fisheries Organisation (ICFO)
- International Health Co-operative Organisation (IHCO)
- International Co-operative Housing Organisation (ICA Housing)
- International Co-operative and Mutual Insurance Federation (ICMIF)
- International Organisation of Industrial, Artisanal and Service Producers' Co-operatives (CICOPA)[9]

NOTES

1. www.ica.coop/aca/index.html.
2. *Ibid.*
3. *Ibid.*
4. *Ibid.*
5. *Annual Report ICA, 2010*
6. www.ica.coop/aca/index.html.
7. *Ibid.*
8. *Ibid.*
9. *Ibid.*

Index